More than Enough

A Brief Guide to the Questions That Arise
After Realizing You Have
More Than You Need

Mike Piper, CPA

Dedication

As always, for you, the reader.

Disclaimer

This book is not intended to be a substitute for personalized advice from a professional financial planner. Nothing contained within this text should be construed as legal or financial advice. The publisher and author make no representation or warranty as to this book's adequacy or appropriateness for any purpose. Similarly, no representation or warranty is made as to the accuracy of the material in this book.

Purchasing this book does not create any client relationship or other advisory, fiduciary, or professional services relationship with the publisher or with the author. *You alone* bear the *sole* responsibility of assessing the merits and risks associated with any financial decisions you make. And it should always be kept in mind that any investment can result in partial or complete loss.

Your Feedback Is Appreciated!

As the author of this book, I'm very interested to hear your thoughts. If you find the book helpful, please let me know! Alternatively, if you have any suggestions of ways to make the book better, I'm eager to hear that, too.

Finally, if you're dissatisfied with your purchase for any reason, let me know, and I'll be happy to provide you with a refund of the current list price of the book (limited to one refund per household).

You can reach me at: mike@simplesubjects.com.

Best Regards,
Mike Piper, CPA

Table of Contents

**Part Four
Finding Professional Assistance**

INTRODUCTION

A New Set of Concerns

In Jack Bogle's 2008 book *Enough: True Measures of Money, Business, and Life*, Bogle shares a story told by author Kurt Vonnegut of a party he attended with fellow-author Joseph Heller. Vonnegut points out to Heller that their billionaire host had likely earned more in the previous day than Heller's classic novel *Catch-22* had earned in the entire time since its publication.

Heller responds, "I've got something he can never have."

To which Vonnegut replies, "What on earth could that be, Joe?"

"The knowledge that I've got enough."

Among people who read personal finance books, many are "super savers"—saving a high percentage of their income through most of their careers. One thing that eventually happens for many such people is that they reach a point at which they realize they have not only saved *Enough*, they have saved *More Than Enough*. Their desired standard of living in retirement is well secured, and it's likely that a major part of the portfolio is eventually going to be left to loved ones and/or charity.

That realization raises a whole list of new questions and concerns. Some of those are financial (e.g., how much can I afford to give away to charity during my lifetime?), and some are non-financial (e.g., how should I communicate my estate plan to my intended heirs?).

This book's goal is to help you answer those questions that arise when you realize you have accumulated—or are on track to accumulate—more than enough.

It often makes sense to start a book with the easy topics first. Pick the low-hanging fruit, allow the reader to build some confidence, and then move on to the more challenging topics.

Unfortunately, that approach doesn't work very well in this case. The financial strategies and tactics are the easy stuff, relatively speaking. But we can't really talk strategies and tactics until you've done the harder work of determining exactly what your goals are.

So, in Part 1 of the book we'll talk through what your goals are with your assets, both during your life as well as upon your death. In Part 2 we'll discuss various financial considerations and strategies for achieving those goals. In Part 3 we'll talk specifically about tax planning strategies that can help achieve those goals. (The common tax advice often needs to be turned on its head if you have significant plans for charitable giving.) And in Part 4 we'll discuss some tips for finding professional assistance, if desired.

Let's Keep This Brief

To be clear, this book is *not* seeking to turn you into an expert on each of the topics discussed. And one of my goals for this book is for it to be relatively brief, so that you can get through the whole thing without feeling overwhelmed. As a result, there's an assortment of advanced topics that aren't included, but which might be relevant to you depending on your circumstances. (For instance, this book includes nothing about creating your own private foundation. Nor does it speak to the many differences in law from one state to another, which may be relevant to estate planning.) There's a whole list of reasons why enlisting professional assistance— such as an estate planning attorney, tax professional, or financial planner—is likely to be prudent. Chapters 18 and 19 provide some guidance on selecting such professionals, if you decide to go that route.

One last note before we get started: throughout the book, I take it as a given that *you care about what happens after you're gone.* When you think about your loved ones and your favorite causes and non-profit organization(s), you care about their success and wellbeing now, but you also care just as much about their success and wellbeing after you're gone, even though you won't be there to see it. If you really do not care—your interest only extends as long as your heartbeat—then this book is not for you. (If that's the case, please take me up on my offer of a refund, as stated on the page before the table of contents.)

PART ONE

What's the Goal?
And Why?

CHAPTER ONE

Do You Have More Than Enough?

In retirement planning, there's constant debate over the topic of what percentage of your portfolio you can safely spend each year.

Unfortunately, no article, book, or study will ever be able to tell you exactly how much you can safely spend each year from your portfolio, for two reasons. Firstly, one household's circumstances can be very different from another household's, in ways that meaningfully change the answer. For instance:

- Will you have an additional source of income kicking in later? For example, if you retire at age 65 and plan to file for Social Security at age 70, it can make sense to spend from savings at a relatively high rate for those five years, if your rate of spending from savings will be very low after Social Security begins.

- How easily could you cut your spending in the future, if necessary? The more easily you could do so, the safer it is to spend at a higher rate now.
- How bad would it be if the portfolio *is* depleted? Or how scary it would be if the portfolio is *nearly* depleted? If Social Security and/or a pension would satisfy your basic needs, a higher spending rate from savings could be reasonable.

And secondly, there's a tremendous amount of uncertainty involved. We don't know how long you will live. We don't know what investment returns you will get. And we don't know whether your future medical costs will be modest, exorbitant, or somewhere in between.

Given this uncertainty and variation among households, suffice to say that this is a major simplification, but a rough guideline is that for any part of the portfolio that you want to last for 30+ years, spending about 3-4% per year is probably reasonable.[1]

---

[1] The following articles may be of interest if you're looking for more discussion on these topics:
https://obliviousinvestor.com/there-is-no-perfect-retirement-spending-strategy/
https://obliviousinvestor.com/an-ideal-retirement-spending-strategy/

Basic division tells us that spending from a portfolio at a rate of 3.33% per year should work for a 30-year retirement, if the portfolio doesn't lose money. Given that, many people are surprised by this low 3-4% figure. After all, the portfolio is probably going to earn *some* investment returns, right?

But the reality is that, because of all the uncertainty involved, many people really *can't* increase the early-in-retirement spending rate very much from there—at least not safely. Because again, if you're spending from a portfolio of risky assets, you have to plan for a case in which 1) you live to a very advanced age, 2) you have massive medical expenses, and 3) your portfolio experiences poor investment returns.

And so we end up with these very low recommended rates of spending from a retirement portfolio.

But here's the important point for our purposes: while you have to *plan* for those three expensive outcomes, the most likely scenario is that you *don't* experience all three of them. Most likely you'll have decent investment returns and you won't live to age 105 in a nursing home. And so, most likely, there will be a significant sum of money left over after you (or after you and your partner) have died. In other words, "enough" ultimately turns out to be "more than enough," most of the time.

And some people spend even less than 3% each year in retirement. I have worked with many clients whose annual spending consists of their Social Security, any pension income, and then only a very modest amount from their portfolio each year (e.g., 1-2%). And they don't particularly *want* to spend any more than that. They've lived in the same home for decades and have no intention to buy a new, more expensive home. (If they're considering a new home, it's likely with aging-related concerns in mind—not just to buy something bigger.) And they're already doing whatever traveling and other spending is necessary to feel satisfied with their lifestyle. In short, they don't anticipate that a major increase in spending would result in a major increase in happiness.

And all of the above leads to an important question: if you're very unlikely to deplete your assets during your lifetime, where should any unspent money go?

Chapter 1 Simple Summary

- Prudent financial planning generally dictates spending at a conservative rate from savings in retirement, because you don't know how long you'll live, you don't know whether you'll incur major medical or long-term care costs, and you don't know what investment returns you'll earn.

- But the most likely scenario is that you don't get financially unlucky in all three of those categories. So if you are spending at a conservative rate, there's a high likelihood that a significant part of the portfolio will remain upon your death.

CHAPTER TWO

Who Gets the Money?

For people with children, it's common for their wills and beneficiary designations on retirement accounts to be written in such a way that the kids (or grandkids) get all the assets remaining at death.

What I've found in working with clients though is that, in many cases, they simply *defaulted* to that decision. (Leaving everything to your children is, after all, the most obvious answer when filling out a beneficiary designation form.) But when they actually gave themselves time to reflect upon the question, they determined that allocating a portion of their estate to various nonprofit organizations (while still allocating, in most cases, a portion to the kids) was more closely aligned with their values and legacy goals.

Most people I speak with tell me that a combination of the two is the answer that ends up feeling right. (Unsurprisingly, people whose loved ones are already financially secure tend to be more likely to leave a greater portion of their assets to charity.)

In working through this question—how much to leave to whom—there are a handful of other questions that are often helpful.

Firstly, do you feel that you *owe* your children an inheritance? And if so, is there any reason to think that it must be a particular portion of your estate? Some people feel an obligation to leave the entire estate to their offspring. In their eyes, to do anything else would be *cheating* their kids. More often though, I hear that there *is* a desire to leave assets to the kids, but the motivation is a *desire to give* rather than a sense of obligation. And that desire to give doesn't necessarily come with a particular price tag (or percentage-of-estate price tag) in the way that those feelings of obligation often do.

Second, are there particular non-profit organizations (or, more broadly, particular charitable causes) that are important to you? Any organizations that have played a major role in your life or causes that are key components of your life's values? (We'll talk more about choosing among specific organizations in Chapter 6.)

It can also be helpful to spend time considering to what extent inheritances of given amounts would meaningfully improve your heirs' lives.

The Consumer Financial Protection Bureau defines financial well-being as the ability to meet your current and ongoing financial obligations, to feel secure in your financial future, and to make choices that allow you to enjoy life.[1] And they provide a survey to assess people's level of financial well-being. It includes questions such as how often the following statements apply to you:

- I could not handle a major unexpected expense.
- Giving a gift for a wedding, birthday, or other occasion would put a strain on my finances for the month.
- I have no money left over at the end of the month.
- Because of my money situation, I feel like I will never have the things I want in life.

For most people reading this book, such circumstances are well into the rear-view mirror. You can give a gift for a birthday, still have money left over at the end of the month, still know that you could handle major unexpected expenses, and still feel that you can "have the things you want in life."

And your children may already be in that position as well—or on track to be in that position.

Would a large inheritance meaningfully improve your heirs' financial well-being? Would it meaningfully improve their *emotional* well-being

---

[1] https://www.consumerfinance.gov/consumer-tools/educator-tools/financial-well-being-resources/data-spotlight-financial-well-being-in-america-2017-2020/

in any way? Or are their financial and emotional well-being already reasonably well satisfied?

If the inheritance *would* meaningfully improve your heirs' lives, would a slightly smaller inheritance be markedly less impactful? For example, if you left 80% to your heirs and 20% to a charity, would your heirs' lives be significantly worse than if they inherited the whole amount?

You may be thinking, "well the kids can just donate it, if they want to." That's true. They can. But the charity (or charities) can actually receive considerably more money if you make this bequest decision during your lifetime, rather than leaving it up to your heirs after your death. For example, if a traditional IRA is left to your kids, they'd have to pay tax on any money they take out of the account, which means they can only give the after-tax amount to charity. If the IRA (or part of it) were instead left directly to the charity, the charity would receive the entire amount in question, tax-free. We'll talk more about these tax planning concepts in Chapter 17.

Allocating Among Recipients

If you have children and grandchildren, and you are trying to choose how to allocate your bequest between the two generations, you may want to spend a few minutes with an online life expectancy calculator. Depending on your health and how old you were when you had kids, you may find that, by the time you die, your kids will likely be in their 60s. Would an inheritance at that age still significantly improve their lives? If not, maybe a larger portion should go to the grandkids or other parties.

As far as allocating among those within a given group, be sure to spend some time carefully reflecting on the exact percentages/amounts. Many people just default to equal percentages to every-body in that group (e.g., 20% to each of my three children, with the remaining 40% going elsewhere).

But fair and equal aren't always the same thing. For instance, what if one of your children has impeded earnings potential due to a disability? Should that child receive a greater portion of any assets left upon your death?

If one of your children provides significant caregiving during your later years, you may want to leave more to that child. (Or consider actually pay-ing them a wage while you're living.)

If you gave significant financial assistance to one of your kids during your lifetime, should that child receive a smaller portion of the inheritance?

Or consider this scenario: you have two chil-dren. One has three children, and the other has no children. During your lifetime you provide signifi-cant financial assistance to the grandkids to help pay for college. Do your two children receive equal portions of the estate? Or is there an adjustment made to reflect the fact that you already helped one child's household?

Reasonable people will come to different answers regarding these questions. And it's possible that what your heirs see as fair is different than what you see as fair. (Regardless of what you think of your children, human nature is to find "fair" to be whatever arrangement most benefits oneself.)

Chapter 2 Simple Summary

- For people with kids, it's common to default to the "everything goes to the kids" estate planning approach. But I find that, when people allow themselves time to think about it, they often decide that some other allocation is more closely aligned with their values and goals.

- If you have kids, would an inheritance meaningfully improve their well-being? And if so, would a somewhat smaller share be significantly less impactful?

- With regard to tax-deferred assets (such as a traditional IRA), leaving them to charity allows the charity to receive the entire amount, whereas an individual beneficiary would only be able to use the amount that's left after paying taxes.

- It's likely that bequests to younger recipients can be more impactful than bequests to recipients who are already financially secure.

- When allocating among individual beneficiaries, be wary of assuming that an equal allocation will necessarily be regarded as fair.

CHAPTER THREE

Talking with Your Kids
Or Other Heirs

For many people, money is a very private topic. And death isn't exactly fun to discuss either. So it's no surprise that many families never get around to having a conversation that combines death and money.

The result is that the (adult) children have no real idea of how much they might inherit.

Why Talk with Your Heirs

From doing individual financial planning work, I can tell you that it presents a dilemma for a household when they believe that they're likely to inherit something, but don't have any idea how much. And in many cases, they don't feel like it's their place to ask.

A household in such a situation often has to plan based on an assumption of zero inheritance. That's the conservative approach, and it's generally prudent. However, your kids might be making real sacrifices right now, based on a no-inheritance assumption, when *you* know that that's not what's going to happen. Maybe they're working a few more years at a job they can't stand. Maybe their kids (your grandkids) are having their education options limited. Point being, even the *knowledge* that they'll be receiving something can improve their lives right now, even if you aren't actually giving them something just yet.

Having this discussion with your children can also result in meaningful tax planning opportunities. If you learn that they intend to donate a portion of the assets, naming the charity in question as a designated beneficiary of a tax-deferred retirement account would allow your heir to not have to pay tax on those assets before donating them.

Common Concerns

Lots of people have concerns about speaking with their heirs about their likely/potential inheritance. For example, you might be concerned that if you reveal your total net assets—and it's much more than your heirs had realized—perhaps you will be pressured for money now. Or perhaps you're afraid that if you mention the possibility of an inheritance to your heirs, it could cause them to become lazy or less ambitious.

Regarding the above concerns, what many people miss is this: if you have had a high-earning career or if your kids know you have been a good saver, your kids are *already expecting* an inheritance, unless they have been given a specific reason to expect otherwise. If those dynamics were likely to exist upon having this discussion, they would probably exist already.

How to Have the Conversation

Many people find that the easiest way to bring the topic up is to refer to a friend or family member's experience—or even just something they've read. ("Remember when Aunt Susan died and it caused big fights between her kids about who got this and who got that? I don't want you all to have that experience.")

You don't have to give exact numbers. And if the amount in question is a percentage of your remaining estate, then there's no way to put a dollar amount on it in advance anyway. But *any* information is more helpful than no information.

In many cases, full disclosure does work well. ("You each get 40%, and that charity we love gets 20%. We don't know how much that will be though. Our assets are about $X right now, but we don't know how our investments will perform, we don't know if we'll have huge medical expenses, and we don't know if we'll each need 15 years of long-term care. And we don't know how long we'll live—you may yourselves be in your 70s before inheriting anything.") Such an approach lets your heirs know as much as can be known, so their curiosity is satisfied and they can plan as well as possible. And you have been as candid as you can be and can feel good about that.

One thing to be prepared for is that people get very serious about money—for obvious reasons. Your kids may get along great all the time. But most of their interactions are probably not financial. And many of the financial interactions that they do have are probably trivial (e.g., reimbursing each other for picking up the carryout at a family get-together).

When the amounts involved are much more significant, resentment and anger can arise where before there was only affection. Such events usually boil down to the fact that one person's version of "fair" may be very different from another person's.

Knowing this might make you reluctant to have this conversation now. But by having the conversation now, you give yourself the opportunity to make adjustments based on input. And, just as important, you have the opportunity to explain your reasoning to them. If the first time they learn of your plans is after your death, you obviously won't be able to make any changes or answer any questions. Any arguments that occur by having the conversation now would likely have occurred anyway—

and without you there to smooth things over or explain your reasoning, what might have been a brief argument can turn into a lasting rift instead.

Chapter 3 Simple Summary

- Any outcomes that you're afraid of happening as a result of discussing your estate plan with your kids would likely happen anyway—or are already happening. (Your kids are likely already expecting an inheritance unless they have a good reason not to expect such. Any fights that happen during the conversation would likely occur later as well, and quite possibly form lasting rifts.)

- By having the conversation now, you give yourself the opportunity to make adjustments based on input. And you give yourself the opportunity to explain your reasoning to them.

PART TWO

Financial Strategies and Considerations

CHAPTER FOUR

Giving and Spending During Your Lifetime

Knowing that, upon your death, you will be leaving assets to loved ones and organizations you care about can bring you a sense of satisfaction during your life. But many people find that it's considerably more enjoyable to donate and give during their lifetimes.

You get to go on a vacation with the kids, instead of them having a "remembering Mom & Dad" vacation. If you get your name on a building or a plaque at a local park, you get to go see it. You get to hear people tell you thanks for donating to their causes.

An all-too-common fact pattern among families in which the parents are financially successful is that the parents do little-to-no donating or giving during their lifetimes. And by the time the parents have died, the "kids" are already retired. And at that point, the inheritance has no major effect on their happiness or standard of living. Donations could have been made earlier. Gifts could have been made earlier, at a time when the kids were younger and more financially challenged.

How Much Can You Afford to Give?

With regard to giving during your lifetime, it immediately raises the question of "how much can I afford to give/donate?" whereas that's obviously a nonissue with regard to bequests. That question, while hard to answer, is at least a question about which there is a bounty of information/discussion—because it's no different than the question of how much you can spend from a portfolio each year. That is, from this standpoint, giving/donating is no different than other spending. (And so again we're left with that "3-4% per year from the portfolio" very rough guideline for somebody early in retirement. Closer to 3% if you're younger. And likely above 4% if you're well into your retirement years.[1])

When spending from a portfolio of risky assets (as opposed to, for example, spending down a bond ladder as the bonds mature) one approach

---

[1] It's worth pointing out that the studies that give us this 3-4% range typically assume no investment costs. If you're paying substantial mutual fund and/or advisory fees, a lower figure is probably wise.

that has become popular is to use the IRS required minimum distribution (RMD) tables to determine the amount to spend each year.

Using RMD tables to calculate a spending amount each year has the advantage of adjusting spending based on your remaining life expectancy (i.e., you can afford to spend a larger percentage of your portfolio per year when you are age 90 than when you're age 60).

While the IRS's "Uniform Lifetime Table" begins at age 72, you can find the prescribed level of spending for earlier ages by using the same underlying method based on life expectancies. Such a strategy would indicate the spending rates shown on the following page for ages 50-100.

As you can see, this is a conservative spending strategy in terms of the initial rate of spending. Some people may want to make adjustments based on differing goals. For example, if you wish to spend at a higher rate during early retirement you could carve out a separate piece of the portfolio to fund such spending. In such cases, that piece of the portfolio should be invested conservatively, given that it will be spent over a short period of time. A similar strategy applies if you plan on a steady level of *overall* spending, but your spending *from the portfolio* will be temporarily high before Social Security kicks in. (That is, you can carve out a portion of the portfolio and invest it in something very safe, in order to satisfy the additional spending from savings during the applicable years. Then you can use the RMD tables to calculate the amount of spending from the rest of the portfolio each year.)

50	2.1%		70	3.4%		90	8.2%
51	2.1%		71	3.5%		91	8.7%
52	2.2%		72	3.6%		92	9.3%
53	2.2%		73	3.8%		93	9.9%
54	2.2%		74	3.9%		94	10.5%
55	2.3%		75	4.1%		95	11.2%
56	2.3%		76	4.2%		96	11.9%
57	2.4%		77	4.4%		97	12.8%
58	2.5%		78	4.5%		98	13.7%
59	2.5%		79	4.7%		99	14.7%
60	2.6%		80	5.0%		100	15.6%
61	2.7%		81	5.2%			
62	2.7%		82	5.4%			
63	2.8%		83	5.6%			
64	2.9%		84	6.0%			
65	2.9%		85	6.3%			
66	3.0%		86	6.6%			
67	3.1%		87	6.9%			
68	3.2%		88	7.3%			
69	3.3%		89	7.8%			

Alternatively, some retirees may want to use a spending strategy such as "RMD percentage, times 1.3." Doing so would bring the initial rate of spending somewhat more in line with recommendations from other strategies. Of course, increasing the initial rate of spending makes the strategy somewhat less safe in terms of portfolio depletion. It also reduces the amount you would leave as a bequest.

Heading Off Future Requests for Gifts

Another frequent concern about giving during your lifetime is that you'll receive frequent requests for further gifts. With respect to charitable contributions, one solution is to use a donor-advised fund to make the donation anonymous. (See Chapter 14 about donor-advised funds.) With gifts to your children or other individual recipients, if you do not plan to make additional gifts going forward, explicitly explaining that the gift is a one-time event can help to prevent misunderstandings.

Gift Taxes

A common concern about giving is whether it will subject you (or the recipients) to gift taxes. In the overwhelming majority of cases, neither the donor nor the recipient will have to pay such tax.

Firstly, gifts are not taxable to the recipient. If anybody must pay a gift tax, it is the person making the gift.

And gifts to your spouse, gifts to charity, gifts to political organizations, and tuition or medical expenses that you pay for somebody else are all specifically excluded (i.e., not subject to gift tax).

In addition, there is an annual exclusion amount ($17,000 as of 2023). Gifts below this amount are not considered taxable gifts. And this annual exclusion amount is per giver, per recipient. For example, if you are married and you have one child who is also married, you could give $17,000 to your child and $17,000 to your child's spouse. And your spouse could do the same, thereby allowing for $68,000 of annual gifts without exceeding the exclusion at all.

And finally, even if you do exceed the annual exclusion, any gift beyond that point isn't immediately going to result in taxes. Rather, that excess amount (known as your **taxable gifts** for the year) then comes out of your lifetime gift/estate tax exclusion amount ($12.92 million as of 2023, though scheduled to be reduced by half as of January 1, 2026). No tax will be paid until your lifetime taxable gifts and your estate collectively exceed that exclusion.

If you have a taxable gift in a given year though (i.e., your gifts to a given recipient in the year exceed the annual exclusion), you will have to file a gift tax return (Form 709) even if you don't have to pay any actual tax.

Student Financial Aid

While a thorough discussion of education planning is beyond the scope of this book, it's worth briefly mentioning that gifts can affect the financial aid that a student would receive. And, more specifically, gifts to the student would generally have a more detrimental effect on that amount of financial aid than gifts to the student's parent(s) would have. If this is relevant to your family, speaking with a financial professional who is an expert in this field is likely worthwhile.

Chapter 4 Simple Summary

- A common pattern among high-earning (or high-saving) households is that they leave large inheritances to their kids...after the "kids" themselves are already retired.

- Relatively modest gifts received early in life are often more impactful than larger inheritances received later in life.

- The amount you can safely spend (or give) from your savings each year depends on your age. One popular approach in financial planning is to base the annual spending on the IRS's required minimum distribution tables.

- In most cases, making gifts will not result in any actual gift tax.

CHAPTER FIVE

Learning to Spend and Give More

After spending decades building habits to *accumulate* savings, many people find it quite challenging to shift to *spending* from savings. That's especially true for people who accumulated their significant savings precisely *by* being very frugal with their spending.

This difficulty in shifting to spending can take many forms.

For instance, you may find yourself tempted to spend only your Social Security benefit and the interest and dividends from your portfolio (i.e., never spend any principal at all). Such a plan is perfectly fine if it allows you to better achieve your goals. The less you spend on yourself, the more you can give to loved ones or charity. But there's no need to feel *scared* about spending from principal, provided that you do so at a reasonable rate. (As discussed in the previous chapter, "reasonable" depends on circumstances—especially your age.)

For other people, they understand on an *intellectual* level that they can afford to spend more. But the part of the brain in charge of emotions is still living in a prior era, when their finances were more constrained. And the result is that spending triggers a variety of unpleasant emotions: anxiety, fear, or regret—even though those responses are no longer warranted by the circumstances.

Or you may find that this difficulty in shifting to spending comes in the form of the "just one more year" syndrome, in which you tell yourself (and maybe the people around you) that you'll retire after just one more year of work—for several years running. No matter the level of assets accumulated, it never *feels* safe enough to terminate that primary source of income.

Similarly, people often hire me to determine whether they can afford to retire. And, in some cases, when I dig into their finances, it becomes clear that, by any reasonable measure, they could have retired years ago.

If any of the above feels familiar, what can you do? How can you become more comfortable with actually *using* your portfolio for its intended purpose?

I propose three things for you to consider: intentional spending, giving, and (depending on the severity of what you're dealing with) meeting with a mental health professional.

Which Types of Spending Are Best?

Simply spending more money is not by any means a sure ticket to greater happiness. But some types of spending are at least more likely to achieve the desired result. There's a wealth of research demonstrating that spending on experiences tends to produce more happiness than spending on material things.[1] But even within that category, the best type(s) of spending vary from one person to another. Many people derive great happiness from travel. For others, travel is just a source of stress. You might find that taking classes is a type of spending that provides fulfillment. Guided experiences can also be a great value (e.g., paying a guide to lead you on an adventurous hike or an architecture tour of your city).

Similarly, any spending that can strengthen existing social connections or build new ones can be a good idea. The incidence of depression spikes in the first few years of retirement, and one of the major contributing factors is the loss of relationships that come from a work environment. Taking a group class can lead to new friendships, as can buying the gear necessary to attend a local meetup that interests you.

---

[1] See, for example, "Spending on doing promotes more moment-to-moment happiness than spending on having" by Amit Kumar, Matthew Killingsworth, Thomas Gilovich.

One category of spending checks off both of the above boxes: experiences with loved ones. Many people find, for instance, that paying for a family trip is some of the best spending they've ever done.

Learning to Give More

A variety of research has shown that people tend to derive more happiness from spending on other people than from spending on themselves.[1]

As with research on spending, there has been research to determine which types of giving are most likely to increase the giver's happiness. Specifically, researchers have found that spending money on others is most likely to increase happiness when the giver can see the difference their gift/spending made, and when they feel a sense of social connection to the person or cause they are helping. (The research also found that it was important that the giver felt that the decision to give was freely chosen, though *most* giving would satisfy that requirement, outside of contrived laboratory contexts.)[2]

Among people who experience negative feelings from major spending (or from thinking about

---

[1] See: "The Emotional Rewards of Prosocial Spending Are Robust and Replicable in Large Samples" by Lara Aknin, Elizabeth Dunn, and Ashley Whillans.
[2] See: "Under What Conditions Does Prosocial Spending Promote Happiness?" by Iris Lok and Elizabeth Dunn.

such spending), many find that giving *doesn't* trigger those same emotions. In addition, giving can have the subconscious effect of sending your brain the message, "I have enough." In other words, giving can unlock the ability to spend on oneself without experiencing negative emotions.

If the thought of giving away money does trigger those same negative feelings for you, I would still encourage you to try giving a small amount—whatever amount feels safe. See what happens; see how you feel after you have done it.

Mental Health Care

It's natural to have some level of nervousness about money. Our finances are a critical piece of our lives, and a major portion of our financial experience is outside of our control (investment returns, changes in tax law, etc.).

But there are some people for whom the level of anxiety they experience is clearly disproportionate to the level of financial risk in their lives. Their needs are very well satisfied—and would still be well satisfied even with a series of bad years in the stock market—and yet they continue to experience intense anxiety about money. If that's the case for you, that doesn't mean there's anything particularly unusual about you. (We *all* have some beliefs and emotional responses that do not entirely align with reality.) It does, however, suggest that some sessions with a mental health professional would likely improve your quality of life.

If the idea of seeking mental health care seems like overkill—or if the concept of mental health care in general strikes you as too "touchy-feely"—I would offer two points to consider. First, mental health best practices are every bit as research-based as various financial concepts that we no longer question (e.g., the fact that mutual funds with low expense ratios tend to outperform funds with high expense ratios). And second, we all have emotions and inner dialogue, and (whether we like it or not) those emotions and inner dialogue influence our actions. So why not seek to have some influence over that dialogue—or at the very least, some awareness of it?

There's considerable research showing cognitive behavioral therapy or mindfulness therapy to be effective methods of reducing anxiety symptoms. Such treatment is very affordable. And it involves little to no risk. (Worst-case scenario is that you waste a bit of time and a modest session fee.)[1]

The goal of such treatments would not be to completely rid yourself of the various money-related beliefs you've built up over the years and all of

---

[1] If you like the idea of some reading you could do on your own, rather than (or prior to) consulting a professional, you may want to read *Mindfulness: An Eight-Week Plan for Finding Peace in a Frantic World* by Mark Williams and Danny Penman.

the emotions you experience around money. For how deeply engrained these things are, that would be impossible. Rather, the goal is simply to slightly lessen their grip over you, in order to improve your overall wellbeing.

Chapter 5 Simple Summary

- Many people find it quite challenging to start spending down their portfolio, after decades of building habits to accumulate assets.

- Some types of spending have been shown to be more likely to result in an increase in happiness than other types of spending. Spending on experiences and spending that helps develop or strengthen social ties are both particularly strong candidates. (The obvious takeaway: spending on memorable experience with loved ones is likely to be some of the best spending you do.)

- Giving (or, more broadly, spending on others) has been shown to be more likely to improve happiness than spending on oneself. Giving can also help by sending your subconscious mind the message, "I have enough."

- If you suspect that you have a level of financial anxiety that is not aligned with your circumstances, meeting with a mental health professional is likely to yield improvements in your quality of life.

CHAPTER SIX

Impactful Charitable Giving

In financial planning, the first step is always a discussion of goals. We can't make well-informed financial decisions before we know what your financial goals are.

The same goes for giving. Step one must be to put time into thinking through exactly what your philanthropic goals are. For most of us, there are plenty of things about the world that we would hope to change. But our resources are limited. And even for those of us who have been financially fortunate, the reality is that giving every dollar we have to a particular philanthropic goal would still not come close to fully solving the problem in question. So we must prioritize.

Effective altruism is a philosophical movement that advocates using a scientific, evidence-based approach to try to determine how to do the most good possible with your charitable giving. A common point of view in the effective altruism movement is that most charitable giving should be directed toward recipients in less economically developed parts of the word, given that a dollar goes further in places in which the most basic needs are not being met.[1]

My own personal view is that climate-related endeavors often have the potential to help the most people, in that, if successful, they help this generation as well as all future generations—to say nothing of the benefit to other animal and plant species.[2]

It's important to consider which philanthropic goal(s) could have the most impact, but an ideal goal would also be something that you're passionate about. There are likely causes that have special meaning to you—research about a particular disease, perhaps, or a particular issue that is a current challenge for your local community. Picking a goal that you are passionate about makes the process much more enjoyable, and it makes it easier to put in the time to research potential recipients and to perform ongoing monitoring to see if you want to continue to give to the organization(s) in question.

---

[1] If you're interested in further reading on this topic, you may want to read *The Life You Can Save* by Peter Singer.

[2] For anybody similarly inclined who is interested in a suggestion, two organizations you may want to consider are the Clean Air Task Force (a nonprofit dedicated to fighting climate change through policy change and technology innovation) and Earthjustice (a nonprofit dedicated to litigating environmental issues).

Selecting Charitable Organizations

Once you have selected your goal(s), there's a compelling case to be made for seeking the maximum impact per dollar given. And that means researching various potential recipients for each goal.

There are various websites that collect and provide information about nonprofit organizations. One such website, GuideStar.org, poses four questions to nonprofit organizations:

1. What is the organization aiming to accomplish?
2. What are the organization's key strategies for making this happen?
3. What are the organization's capabilities for doing this?
4. What have they accomplished so far, and what's next?

Even if an organization hasn't provided that information on GuideStar, those are great questions for you to ask the organization—or to research on your own via their website and other publications.

On GuideStar or similar websites, you can also view the organization's Form 990—the annual tax return filed with the IRS—if you're so inclined.

Overhead Costs and Program Costs

When donating, many people have an intense focus on overhead costs as compared to costs that directly pay for the organization's programs. This focus can come in the form of:

- Donating only to organizations whose overhead costs are a very low percentage of overall costs or
- Making donations that are restricted as to use (i.e., the dollars cannot be used for overhead costs).

In my opinion, such a focus is often misguided, for a few reasons.[1]

Firstly, overhead often includes salaries for people in a range of critical positions in the organization. We obviously don't want our donated dollars going to pay for exorbitant salaries. But it is important for compensation levels to at least be in the ballpark of what a person could get outside of the nonprofit sector. Otherwise, many of the organization's employees will be either a) people who couldn't actually get (or keep) those other jobs or b) great employees who only stick around for a short while, before the financial sacrifice becomes too much and they go elsewhere.

---

[1] If you're interested in additional reading on this topic, I'd recommend *Giving Done Right* by Phil Buchanan.

Second, the systems, technology, and people that are needed to track and evaluate the effectiveness of a given program would likely themselves be considered overhead.

Third, the data itself is unreliable in some cases, as two different sources may classify the same cost differently.

And finally, in many cases, it just doesn't make sense to compare financial ratios of two meaningfully different organizations. For example, imagine two organizations, both of which seek to serve the homeless population in your community. The first is an organization that lobbies for policy changes at the state and local level. The organization has no physical office, as all of the employees work from home. The second organization is a local soup kitchen. Of the two, the lobbying organization is very likely to have lower overhead costs, as they have no rent to pay. But does that necessarily mean that it's a more effective organization or that it's using donated funds more efficiently?

One context in which it does make sense to pay attention to overhead costs: if you're regularly being wined and dined by a charity to which you donate, that's effectively coming right out of your contributions. Better to have the money go toward the goals that you and this charity share. If you're concerned about unnecessary costs, don't make yourself one.

Restricted vs. Unrestricted Gifts

When you donate to a non-profit organization, you can specify that the money can only be used for a certain purpose. Some people feel that making such "restricted" gifts ensures that their donated money doesn't go to waste, because it will only be spent directly on programs rather than overhead costs.

But, as discussed above, it's not as if money spent on non-program costs is by definition wasted. A certain level of overhead cost is necessary in order to keep the programs running.

Rather than making restricted donations, I would suggest the following approach: if you trust the organization to use donated money wisely, make an unrestricted gift. Allow the charity to make the decision about how to use the resources most effectively. And if you *don't* trust the organization to use the money wisely, don't give to that organization in the first place!

Measuring Performance

When investing, we can check our account balances any time we want. We can calculate rates of return. We have meaningful metrics, we don't have to do much work to calculate those metrics, and those metrics are available on an up-to-the-minute basis.

Philanthropy isn't like that. You can measure how much you're giving, but it's hard (often impossible) to go from there to "what impact did it have?"

It often takes serious thought to determine an appropriate metric for measuring success toward a given philanthropic goal. And even after putting in that work, those metrics generally aren't comparable from one philanthropic goal to another (e.g., whatever metric you use to track success toward improving elementary-level education is almost certainly not going to be useful for tracking success in achieving environmental protections).

In addition, for most of the problems people seek to address through philanthropy, progress is slow. From the time a program is first put in place, it's often years before there's any data about effectiveness. And even then, there's often no way to know where the metrics would stand without the program at all (e.g., perhaps progress toward the goal would have been made due to other factors).

In most cases, as individual donors, the closest we can come to knowing we're making a difference is to be confident that a) the organization is making a difference and b) we are contributing to the organization. So, for any organizations to which you give, it's worth knowing: what metrics *does* the organization track? And what evidence does it have of progress? For the reasons discussed above, the evidence shouldn't need to be ironclad scientific proof. But there should be some compelling evidence.

Chapter 6 Simple Summary

- The first step in planned giving is to define your goal(s). Some goals may be more impactful (or more impactful per dollar given) than other goals, but it's also important to choose goals that you're passionate about.

- Before giving to an organization, take time to learn what specifically it aims to accomplish, how exactly it intends to do that, and what it has achieved so far.

- An overwhelming focus on overhead costs can be detrimental to achieving many legitimate philanthropic goals. For some types of charitable work, overhead costs are simply going to be higher than for other types of charitable work, even if the organization is run very efficiently.

- If you trust an organization to spend its resources wisely, I encourage you to make unrestricted gifts rather than restricted. And if you don't trust the organization to spend its resources wisely, find a different organization to give to!

CHAPTER SEVEN

Impactful Investing

When it comes to investing, the default assumption is that the goal is to achieve as much return as possible, without taking on more risk than you can handle.

Increasingly, however, people seek to have their portfolios work toward multiple goals. That is, they hope that in addition to earning worthwhile returns, they can achieve other non-financial goals as a result of how their dollars are invested.

A common way to invest these days is via an "ESG" mutual fund, which excludes various companies, depending on their practices in environmental, social, and governance (E, S, and G) categories. The idea is that, if enough people choose to exclude these stocks from their portfolio, the stock's price will decline (due to lower demand), and the firm's management (whose pay is often based on the performance of the stock) will be persuaded to make different decisions.

However, there are two problems with such a strategy. First, there are plenty of investors (not just individual investors but also mutual funds, hedge funds, etc.) who are eager to buy the socially or ethically undesirable stocks at bargain prices—thereby driving the prices right back up.[1]

Second, by choosing *not* to own shares of a particular business, you *give up* a very direct means of influencing that business. The owners (shareholders) of a corporation have power. Shareholders have the right to vote on important issues facing the business. Shareholders have the right to speak at the corporation's shareholder meetings and argue for or against various courses of action. And they have the right to vote on membership of the company's board of directors.

If I wanted to change a company's behavior, excluding that company from my portfolio—thereby giving up all of those rights—is *precisely the opposite* of how I would go about it.

If a fund's way of being socially responsible is simply to exclude certain stocks from the fund, it is giving up its power to vote to change the behaviors of those companies. My own preference is for a low-cost fund that owns all publicly-traded firms (i.e., an index fund or ETF) and which votes to make the changes I want to see. I do not want a fund that

---

[1] For a more technical discussion of this topic, see the paper "The Impact of Impact Investing" by Jonathan Berk and Jules H. van Binsbergen.

goes out of its way to give up a major source of influence over precisely the companies I would most like to influence.

There is at least one fund company that is taking this shareholder activism-based approach. I am reluctant to name specific funds or specific fund companies though (either as recommendations for or against), because this is an area that's very much in flux as of this writing. As soon as I put something in a printed publication, it's likely to become obsolete soon thereafter. Fund companies are receiving major pressure regarding their policies for how they vote their shares, and their policies are shifting as a result.

In addition, your view of what shareholder activism should look like (i.e., how you would want a fund manager to vote underlying shares on your behalf) may be very different from my own view.

For the funds you own that hold stocks—or any stock fund you're considering buying—I would encourage you to look into how the fund manager votes its shares. You can find a fund's policies and procedures for voting its shares in the fund's Statement of Additional Information. The Statement of Additional Information should be available on the fund company's website, typically on the same page where you would find the fund's prospectus. You might find that the fund's official voting policy is quite different than what is implied in the fund's marketing materials.

Relatedly, I would caution you not to assume that a fund votes its shares in a certain way just because of the fund's name. One well-known fund company has received flack in the last few years for its ESG fund that has a track record of consistently voting *against* ESG-related shareholder proposals.[1]

Chapter 7 Simple Summary

- For any mutual funds that you own or are considering buying, I would encourage you to pay attention to the fund's policies for voting the shares that it owns, to check whether those policies align with your values. And, specifically, I would encourage you to read the official policies in the fund's Statement of Additional Information.

- I would encourage you to be skeptical of the idea that you can significantly influence a company's behavior by choosing not to be a shareholder.

---

[1] If you're *really* interested in digging into this research, you can look up for yourself exactly how a given fund has voted on specific proposals. To find this information, you'll want to visit the SEC's "EDGAR" database, navigate to the search for mutual funds, look up the fund in question, and locate its Form NP-X.

CHAPTER EIGHT

Reassess Your Asset Allocation

Famed financial writer William Bernstein has a saying that, "if you've won the game, why keep playing?" Point being, if your goals are currently satisfied—and a significant decline in your portfolio value would put your goals at risk—then there's no sense in using a risky allocation for your portfolio. Why take risk when you don't need it and it would put your goals in jeopardy?

On the other hand, for some people in the "more than enough" boat, even a significant portfolio decline wouldn't put their standard of living at risk. That is, if you're already spending from your portfolio at a very low rate, a significant decline would not be enjoyable, but it wouldn't put you in any meaningful danger.

So an important question to answer is: how badly would things have to go before your standard of living and other goals are impacted?

If it becomes clear to you at some point that your standard of living is really not at risk from market volatility—and the bulk of your portfolio is going to end up going to other parties eventually—the decisions that make sense for most people do not necessarily make sense for you. You're no longer investing this money primarily for your own retirement but rather primarily on behalf of your kids, other loved ones, charities, etc.

In such cases, you may find that it makes sense to think of your portfolio as an endowment rather than a personal retirement portfolio. That typically means using an equity-oriented asset allocation, such as 70% in stocks and 30% in fixed-income, in order to allow for modest spending from the portfolio while also, hopefully, providing for inflation-adjusted growth over time. It also typically means using a static asset allocation, to which you rebalance periodically (e.g., quarterly or annually), rather than adjusting over time based on your age.

Conversely, when you no longer *need* a high rate of return from your portfolio, you can choose a low level of risk, if you prefer. Either decision—or anywhere in between—can be reasonable.

Whenever discussing allocation for a portfolio, I think it's important to note that asset allocation is not a precise science. There is no single allocation that is *perfect* for a particular household.

Rather, there are numerous allocations that would be *perfectly fine*. A portfolio only has to satisfy a handful of conditions in order to be good enough:

1. It must be diversified (e.g., no massive holding of one single stock).
2. It must have a level of risk that's suitable for the household's circumstances.
3. It must be low-cost. That is, it should not include any mutual funds with high expense ratios. (Ideally, expense ratios should be kept below 0.1%, or possibly slightly higher if using an "all-in-one" fund such as a target-date fund.)
4. It must be tax-efficient (i.e., no tax-inefficient funds in taxable brokerage accounts).
5. It must be simple enough to manage without difficulty.

Chapter 8 Simple Summary

- If your goals are currently satisfied but a significant decline in your portfolio would put them in jeopardy, then you have little need for risk in your portfolio and a compelling reason not to take on a lot of risk.

- Conversely, if it becomes clear that your standard of living is not at risk and your portfolio is no longer primarily a retirement portfolio but rather a portfolio for other parties (e.g., your offspring and/or charity), the asset allocations that typically make sense for a retirement portfolio may no longer make sense for you. If you prefer, you may want to begin to think of your portfolio as an endowment rather than as a personal retirement portfolio, which would generally mean using a static, stock-oriented allocation.

- If a portfolio is diversified, has a level of risk that's appropriate, is low-cost and tax-efficient, and is simple enough to manage, it's a "good enough" portfolio.

CHAPTER NINE

Trusts

There are some cases in which assets should not be left directly to one or more of your intended heirs (e.g., because the heir is a minor, disabled, or simply has a history of making poor decisions).

Or consider this scenario: after your death, your surviving spouse remarries. And, when your surviving spouse later dies, all of the assets that you currently think of as your assets are ultimately left to the new spouse. And when that new spouse dies, all of the assets go to his or her kids rather than to your kids or other intended beneficiaries.

A trust is the solution to situations such as the above.

There are many different types of trusts, each of which serves a particular purpose. The basic idea though is that a trust is a legal entity which can own assets. Sometimes trusts are used for tax planning purposes. In many cases though, the purpose is to allow the person who created the trust to exert some control over how their assets will be managed after their death or incapacitation. That is, somebody can create a trust, fund it with assets, and write the terms of the trust in such a way as to stipulate certain requirements as to how the assets will be invested or spent—and then those rules will have to be followed even after the person who created the trust dies or becomes incapacitated.

With trusts, it's important to get guidance from an attorney who specializes in estate planning. If the attorney is not a tax expert, it's critical that the firm has somebody on their team who *can* provide expert tax guidance, as there are both income tax and estate/gift tax considerations involved with trusts.

In order to understand the various purposes for a trust, you first need to know a bit of terminology.

Parties to a Trust

A trust involves three parties: the grantor, the beneficiary, and the trustee.

- The **grantor** (sometimes called the **donor** or **settlor**) is the party who defines the terms (rules) of the trust, transfers property to the trust, and, usually, retains the right to change the trust until his or her death.

- The **beneficiary** (or beneficiaries) is the party for whose benefit the assets in the trust are held/managed.
- The **trustee** is the party in charge of managing the trust (e.g., making investment decisions, distributing assets to the beneficiary when applicable, and fulfilling any administrative requirements). The trustee owes a fiduciary duty to the beneficiary (i.e., a duty to put the beneficiary's interests above the trustee's own interests). And the trustee must manage the trust in such a way that is in keeping with the terms of the trust.

These parties may be actual human persons, or they may be legal entities. For instance, you could name a law firm or CPA firm as the trustee to a trust. And it's common to name a non-profit organization as a beneficiary of a trust.

The trust may also designate somebody as a **successor trustee**, to take over when the initial trustee dies, becomes incapacitated, or relinquishes the role.

The trust may also designate one or more parties as **secondary beneficiaries** (also referred to as **contingent beneficiaries**), for whose benefit the assets would be managed if the primary beneficiary has died.

Another important point is that, while there are three parties to a trust, one person may actually be in multiple roles—or even all three roles.

EXAMPLE: Collin is the grantor of a trust (i.e., he funded it with his own assets). The trust is set up so that Collin is also the trustee and beneficiary while he is still alive, with his sister named as the successor trustee and his children named as the secondary beneficiaries.

One way to think about this is that before Collin created the trust, he had various rights in his assets. When he created and funded the trust, he transferred some of the rights in his assets to himself as the grantor, some to himself as trustee, and some to himself as beneficiary. Consequently, he retained all the rights in his assets that he held before the trust was created, but he now holds them in different capacities. In so doing, he creates a mechanism for others to act in the various capacities in the future.

As time passes, his sister may take over management of the trust as successor trustee when, for example, Collin becomes unable to manage his assets on his own. In addition, at Collin's death, if his sister hadn't already, she would become successor trustee and his children, the contingent beneficiaries, would become entitled to the benefits of the trust.

Note that there is no successor grantor because the main power given to the grantor is to change the trust. However, when the grantor dies, a trust becomes irrevocable, and cannot be changed.

More Trust Terminology

A trust can be an inter vivos trust or a testamentary trust. An **inter vivos trust** is created by the grantor during his or her lifetime, whereas a **testamentary trust** is created at the time of the grantor's death. That is, with a testamentary trust, the grantor's will provides for the trust to be created and funded upon his or her death.

A trust can be revocable or irrevocable. With a **revocable trust**, the grantor can change the terms of the trust (or even terminate it completely) as long as he/she is still alive and of sound mind. With an **irrevocable trust**, there are some exceptions, but changes generally cannot be made once the trust has been created.[1]

More Trust Usage Examples

With the above terminology discussion out of the way, we can go through a few examples of cases in which a trust would be useful.

---

[1] The fact that you cannot make changes to an irrevocable trust is not, in itself, beneficial. But there are certain goals that can only be achieved with irrevocable trusts. For instance, if somebody sues you, they often will not be able to access assets in an irrevocable trust. Similarly, as mentioned later in this chapter, irrevocable trusts can be helpful for minimizing estate taxes.

EXAMPLE: Susie is a widow with three adult children (two daughters and a son). Her son has a long history of making poor financial decisions. In Susie's will, rather than leaving 1/3 of her assets to each of her children outright, she leaves 1/3 to each of the daughters, and she leaves the remaining 1/3 to a trust. Susie names her son as the beneficiary of the trust, and she names her attorney as the trustee. This way her son still receives the benefits of the assets, but somebody else (the trustee) will be choosing how to invest and spend the assets.

EXAMPLE: Luther and Harriette are married, in their 60s. Harriette has two adult children from a prior marriage. Luther does not get along with Harriette's children. Harriette is concerned that if she dies before Luther and her assets are simply left to Luther at her death, he will ultimately disinherit her children. As a result, Harriette provides in her will for a testamentary trust to be created upon her death and for her assets to be placed into that trust. The terms of the trust are that Luther will receive the income from the assets while he is alive, and then the assets will be left to her children upon Luther's death.

EXAMPLE: Nigel and Veronica have an adult son who is disabled. The son is currently receiving Social Security disability benefits. And because of his low level of income and assets, he also qualifies for Supplemental Security Income (SSI) and Medicaid.

If they simply leave their assets to him outright, he would lose eligibility for SSI and Medicaid. Instead, they create a special needs trust, which will receive their assets upon the death of the second spouse. Their son is named as beneficiary of the trust, and a trusted CPA is named as the trustee. Because the son has no control over the assets in the trust, it will not disqualify him from receiving SSI or Medicaid. The trustee will not be allowed to outright give the assets to the son, but the assets can be used for a variety of purposes for the benefit of the son.

Trusts are sometimes used to reduce potential estate tax costs. One of the ways to do this is to transfer assets to an irrevocable trust (thereby removing the assets from the grantor's taxable estate), often while maintaining some current benefit (e.g., the right to take income from the assets for a period of years). By transferring assets now, the grantor will often have a taxable gift, but a significant advantage is that the gift is at today's value, rather than at some more highly appreciated value at the date of the grantor's death. There are many different variations on this concept though (e.g., intentionally defective grantor trusts, qualified personal residence trusts, charitable remainder trusts, etc.).

Another common use of trusts is simply to avoid probate. Assets that are placed in a trust do not have to go through probate upon the death of the grantor, because the terms of the trust (rather than state probate laws) govern how the assets are transferred. In some cases, avoiding probate can result in significant savings in terms of costs and time. (The cost of probate and administrative hassle involved vary considerably by state.)

In other cases, people may want to avoid having their assets go through probate for the sake of privacy. Probate records, including the will and estate inventory, are generally public information, whereas trusts are not.

Note though that if your goal for a trust is to have assets pass to beneficiaries without having to go through probate, it will be important that the trust is an inter vivos trust rather than a testamentary trust. Testamentary trusts do not avoid probate. (They come into being *as a part of probate*, via the will.)

Responsibilities as Trustee

The trustee of a trust has certain responsibilities and powers, which should be spelled out in the trust document.

One of those responsibilities is that the trustee has a fiduciary duty to the beneficiaries of the trust. That is, the trustee must manage the assets in a prudent way for the benefit of the beneficiaries, and the trustee must put the interests of the beneficiaries above the trustee's own interests (other than to the extent that the trustee is a beneficiary).

The details vary by state law, but the trustee generally has a duty to keep the beneficiaries informed as to the administration of the trust. This often includes providing (at least) annual statements as to the trust's assets, liabilities, income, expenses, and distributions. If/when the trust is closed, the trustee should send each beneficiary a record of all the major actions taken as trustee, including distributions made.

As with an estate, a trust is a taxable entity.[1] If a trust has gross income of $600 or more for the year (or any taxable income more than zero), the trustee must file a Form 1041 reporting (and potentially paying tax on) that income.

If you are trustee of a trust, it's important to keep records of your actions in that role. Document any significant actions that you take (investment decisions, distributions from the trust, etc.) as well as your reason for those actions.

Professional Trustees

If you have (or plan to create) a trust, one important decision you'll have to make is whether to name a

---

[1] There are some exceptions while the grantor is still alive. That is, with some types of trusts, the trust's income is simply treated as if it were the grantor's income. However, once the grantor dies, the trust will be considered a separate taxpayer going forward.

family member or a professional entity as the trustee (or as the successor trustee, if you're naming yourself as the original trustee).

The primary benefit of naming a family member as trustee (or multiple family members, as co-trustees) is that doing so will avoid some costs. Professional services are not free of course. An additional potential benefit is that a family member will have better knowledge of family dynamics, which can be helpful in some cases.

There are, however, significant points in favor of hiring a professional trustee.

Firstly, having a professional serve as trustee can prevent conflict in some cases, as the trustee will be an outsider, impartial among beneficiaries. And even if conflict isn't avoided, it can be nice if the ill will is at least directed toward an outsider rather than toward a family member. (In some cases, the beneficiary of a trust comes to see the trustee as "the person who keeps me from getting to my money." If the trustee and beneficiary are family, this can create permanent rifts.)

Second, naming a family member as trustee often imposes a significant burden on that person, in terms of time, stress, and potentially family conflict. And that burden may last for years.

Third, a professional trustee will have relevant skills and knowledge (e.g., investment experience), which a family member may not have.

And finally, hiring a professional trustee will generally provide some level of oversight. That is, the firm providing the service generally will have some level of internal controls to prevent theft, mismanagement, etc. In contrast, if you name, for example, your adult son as the trustee of a trust with your adult disabled daughter as the beneficiary, there may be no meaningful oversight—nobody checking to make sure that your son is performing his responsibilities appropriately.

Chapter 9 Simple Summary

- A trust is a legal entity that can own property. There are many types of trusts, each with a different purpose, but the most common uses of trusts are to avoid probate, minimize estate taxes, or exert some control over a pool of assets after the grantor dies or becomes incapacitated.

- The grantor/donor is the party who creates the trust, defines its terms, and funds the trust with assets.

- The trustee is the party in charge of managing the trust.

- The beneficiary is the party for whom the trust's assets are managed.

- The trustee of a trust has a fiduciary duty to the trust's beneficiaries.

- Naming a professional as trustee of a trust does result in some additional costs, relative to naming a family member. But it also adds meaningful safeguards and may help to prevent family conflict.

CHAPTER TEN

Asset Protection

Taking steps to guard your assets from potential lawsuits is known as **asset protection**.

Before discussing specific asset protection strategies, it's worth noting two overall points.

Firstly, the applicable law varies meaningfully from one state to another. So if this is an area of concern for you, guidance from a local attorney is likely to be valuable.

Second, one of the most productive things you can do with regard to asset protection is not any sort of creative legal strategy but rather to reduce the risks in your life. For example, if you have a teenage driver in your home, consider paying for qualified driving instruction, beyond what they have already received. It reduces the risk of harm to your loved one as well as everybody around them on the road. And, if that wasn't reason enough, it also reduces your financial risk.

After taking steps to reduce the risk in your life, the next box to make sure you have checked is appropriate insurance coverage. Liability insurance is relatively inexpensive, easy to purchase, and effective. If you're concerned about asset protection, it's generally a good idea to:

- Choose the maximum liability coverage on your homeowners/renters insurance.
- Choose the maximum liability coverage on your auto policies.
- Purchase personal liability ("umbrella") coverage.
- Purchase professional liability coverage, if you're not retired and you work in a field where people get sued.
- Make sure that you are covered by directors and officers insurance, if you volunteer on the Board of any non-profit organizations.

Retirement accounts provide an additional source of asset protection. Assets in an employer-sponsored retirement plan covered by the Employee Retirement Income Security Act (ERISA), such as a 401(k) plan, are completely protected from creditors in bankruptcy proceedings.[1] Similarly, assets

---

[1] Single-participant 401(k) plans for self-employed people, often known as "solo 401(k)" or "individual 401(k)" plans are not covered by ERISA and do not receive this protection.

in a **rollover IRA** (i.e., an IRA funded only by dollars rolled over from an ERISA-covered plan) have unlimited protection in bankruptcy proceedings under federal law. In contrast, for any IRA to which you have made a contribution, federal protection in bankruptcy is only up to a limit ($1,512,350 as of 2023). Because of this limit, it can make sense *not* to combine a rollover IRA with another traditional IRA. Inherited IRAs are not protected under federal law. In addition to the above federal protection, many states extend additional protection to IRA assets.

Many states also offer some degree of creditor protection for any cash value in a life insurance policy or deferred annuity. I would encourage you to tread carefully though: be sure that your state does offer such protection and that you would benefit from such protection, because such insurance policies are *not* usually a great value from a purely investment standpoint.

Trusts can be helpful asset protection tools as well. Specifically, assets that have been transferred to an irrevocable trust will typically not be accessible by anybody suing you. Though, with the trust being irrevocable, you do lose some of the flexibility that you have when you simply own the assets in your own name. You'll also want to make sure that the transfer would not be considered a fraudulent conveyance. A **fraudulent conveyance** is when you transfer an asset to another party, with the intent to put that asset beyond the reach of a known creditor. In other words, if you have already been sued or you believe you're likely to be sued, a transfer of assets to another party (including an irrevocable trust) is likely to be considered a fraudulent conveyance and would probably be reversed by a bankruptcy court.

In some cases, forming a business entity (e.g., LLC, corporation, or family limited partnership) can provide some asset protection. However, many people overestimate the protection provided by such entities, for a few reasons. Firstly, if there's no genuine business reason for the entity (i.e., no actual ongoing business being operated), it's unlikely to have much value in protecting your assets, because a court will be much more likely to "pierce the corporate veil" in the event of a lawsuit. Second, such business entities don't protect you from your own **torts** (i.e., wrongful acts that lead to liability), because you always have personal liability for any torts that you commit. Finally, you will have personal liability for any contracts that you sign in a personal capacity (rather than as an agent of the business).

One last strategy to consider: giving. Any money that you have donated to charity or given to other loved ones will generally not be reachable in a lawsuit. (Again, fraudulent conveyances would be an exception.)

Chapter 10 Simple Summary

- One useful asset protection strategy is to reduce the risk in your life.

- Much of the relevant law in the field of asset protection varies by state, so guidance from a local attorney can be very valuable.

- Making sure you have appropriate liability insurance coverage is an easy, relatively inexpensive way to reduce your risk.

- Retirement accounts also provide some asset protection, though the details vary by type of account as well as by state.

- For some people with asset protection concerns, transferring assets to an irrevocable trust can be beneficial.

- If you operate a business, an entity such as an LLC can provide valuable protection.

- If you're worried that you're a target for lawsuits because you have a lot of assets, consider giving some of those assets away.

PART THREE

Tax Strategies

CHAPTER ELEVEN

Qualified Charitable Distributions

The recognition that much of your portfolio will ultimately go to other parties brings up a list of new tax planning considerations. And, for people with charitable intentions, much of the common tax planning advice needs to be revised considerably.

For instance, many people with "more than enough" find the following to be true:

1. They don't intend to spend their whole required minimum distribution (RMD) each year, and
2. They're concerned about the taxes they'll have to pay once RMDs kick in.

If that sounds like you, and you aren't opposed to donating some money to charity, qualified charitable distributions are the answer.

A **qualified charitable distribution** (QCD) is a distribution from a traditional IRA directly to a charitable organization (i.e., the check is made out directly to the organization rather than to you). Unlike most distributions from a traditional IRA, QCDs are not taxable as income. And QCDs count toward your required minimum distribution for the year in which you take the QCD. QCDs are limited to $100,000/year (per spouse, if you're married).[1]

To qualify for qualified charitable distributions you must be at least age 70.5. (Yes, it really is age 70.5. The legislation that increased the age for RMDs did not change the age for QCDs.)

Qualified charitable distributions work on a calendar year basis. That is, there's no "I'm doing this in March of 2024, and I want it to count for 2023" option as there is for contributions to an IRA.

Another important point about qualified charitable distributions is that they cannot be taken from an employer-sponsored plan such as a 401(k) or 403(b). They must come specifically from traditional IRAs. (This can be a point in favor of rolling assets from an employer-sponsored plan to a traditional IRA.)

Qualified charitable distributions are generally more tax-efficient than taking a normal distribution, having it included in your taxable income, and then donating the money. In that second case

---

[1] Beginning in 2024, this $100,000 limit will receive annual inflation adjustments.

(taking a taxable distribution, then donating the money), you get an itemized deduction. With a QCD, the donated amount is completely excluded from income which means you can still use the standard deduction in the year in question and still receive a tax benefit from your charitable giving. It also means that your adjusted gross income (AGI) is lower, which can result in other tax savings, because various other deductions and credits are based on your level of AGI.

One final note about QCD rules: a donor-advised fund (discussed in Chapter 14) cannot be the recipient of a qualified charitable distribution.

Chapter 11 Simple Summary

- A qualified charitable distribution is a distribution from a traditional IRA directly to a charitable organization (other than a donor-advised fund).

- QCDs are excluded from your gross income, but they still count toward your required minimum distribution for the year in which you take the QCD.

- QCDs are limited to $100,000 per year (per spouse, if you're married). This $100,000 limit is scheduled to start receiving annual inflation adjustments beginning in 2024.

- You must be at least age 70.5 in order to take a qualified charitable distribution.

- For people with charitable intentions who don't intend to spend their entire RMD in a given year and who are concerned about the tax bill they'll face on their RMDs, qualified charitable distributions are an excellent solution. The overall result is that you were able to claim a deduction when you put the money into the account, the money grew tax-free over time while it remained in the account, and now it comes out tax-free as well.

CHAPTER TWELVE

Donating Appreciated Taxable Assets

When you donate taxable assets (i.e., assets that are *not* in any account with special tax treatment such as an IRA) that have gone up in value and that you have owned for longer than one year, you get to claim an itemized deduction for the current market value of the asset and you do not have to pay tax on the appreciation.

When donating taxable property that you have held for one year or less, your itemized deduction is limited to your cost basis in the property.

EXAMPLE: Carmen owns shares of stock that she purchased 18 months ago for a total of $19,000. The shares are currently worth $25,000. If she donates them, she will receive an itemized deduction for their fair market value ($25,000).

If, however, she had only owned the shares for 6 months, she would only be entitled to a deduction equal to her cost basis ($19,000).

In other words, when donating appreciated taxable assets that you have held for longer than one year, there are two potential sources of tax savings. Firstly, you get an itemized deduction for the donation. And secondly, you do not have to pay tax on the appreciation.

Chapter 12 Simple Summary

- Donating taxable assets that you have owned for longer than one year and which have gone up in value is often a tax-advantageous strategy. It allows you to claim an itemized deduction equal to the value of the donated property, while also avoiding taxation on the appreciation.

CHAPTER THIRTEEN

Deduction Bunching

A common tax planning strategy is to "bunch" itemized deductions into a given year. The idea is to rack up a whole bunch of itemized deductions in one year, and then in the next few years have little to no itemized deductions—and therefore take the standard deduction in those years—then repeat the process every few years.

EXAMPLE: Isra and Ben are married. They normally contribute approximately $10,000 to charity each year. And they pay at least $10,000 of state income tax each year (i.e., the maximum deductible amount of state taxes). They have no other itemized deductions.

In such a situation, Isra and Ben gain no value from their itemized deductions at all, because they total $20,000, which is less than the standard deduction for a married couple who file jointly ($27,700 in 2023).

After Isra and Ben learn about deduction bunching, they adjust their approach. Instead of donating $10,000 each year, they donate $50,000 every fifth year. This way, they can take $60,000 of itemized deductions in that year (i.e., their charitable contributions plus $10,000 of state income tax), and they can still use the standard deduction in the other four years.

An important point to note when bunching donations is that your itemized deduction for charitable contributions in a given year can be limited to certain percentages of your income, depending on what type of property you are donating and what type of organization you're donating to. (See IRS Publication 526 for more details.)

It's not as easy to control the timing of other itemized deductions, but the concept applies to them as well. For instance, medical expenses are usually only deductible if they exceed 7.5% of your adjusted gross income. Bunching medical expenses into a given year may make it easier to exceed that threshold, which would be especially useful if it's in the same year in which you make the every-several-years donation. (Bunching medical expenses often makes sense anyway, when possible, given the way that insurance deductibles and out-of-pocket maximums work.)

Chapter 13 Simple Summary

- By "bunching" itemized deductions into certain years, you may be able to actually get some tax savings from them, when you would otherwise just claim the standard deduction every year.

- One of the easiest ways to bunch itemized deductions is by bunching donations to charity (e.g., making one large donation every several years or every few years, rather than smaller donations every year).

CHAPTER FOURTEEN

Donor-Advised Funds

A **donor-advised fund** is a nonprofit entity, often run by a financial institution (e.g., Vanguard, Fidelity, or Schwab). When you contribute money to the fund, it counts as a charitable contribution for tax purposes (i.e., you get an itemized deduction). And money you contribute to the fund goes into an account over which you have (limited) control. The money is no longer your money—you can't take it out and spend it on groceries. But you maintain control of how it is invested. And at any time you can choose to have distributions ("grants") made from the account to one or more charities of your choosing. (Such grants have no tax impact for you, because you're not actually a party to those transactions. They are transactions between the fund and the ultimate charities.)

There are three main reasons why you might benefit from using a donor-advised fund:

1. You can get the tax deduction now, without yet needing to figure out how much you want to give to which charities.
2. They provide anonymity, if desired.
3. They make it easier to donate securities (e.g., shares of mutual funds or stocks).

Note that none of these is a tax benefit.

Some companies that run donor-advised funds promote them as if they offer tax benefits, when in reality it's just the same tax benefits that come from charitable contributions in general. That is, you don't save any taxes with a donor-advised fund that you wouldn't have saved by simply donating directly to the ultimate charitable recipient(s) instead of donating to the donor-advised fund.

The benefits offered by donor-advised funds are *administrative* benefits. But these administrative benefits can be valuable.

Deduction Now, Decide Recipient Later

Just to reiterate, once you've contributed money to a donor-advised fund, that money is no longer your money. You cannot take it back out to spend on groceries. You cannot distribute the money to your nephew, even if he really needs it. And the money does not go to your kids when you die. So, in that sense, the donation decision is final as of the date that you contribute to the fund.

But there might be years when, based on your budget and tax planning, you decide that you want to make charitable donations of $X. And it's often the case that this decision is made close to year-end (i.e., after you have a good idea as to your various amounts of income/deductions). And you might not, right at that moment, want to have to figure out exactly how many dollars go to which charities. So you can make a contribution to the donor-advised fund, and then take your time with determining the ultimate recipients of the dollars. (Though the ultimate recipients *do* have to be charitable organizations.)

Many people use donor-advised funds to implement a deduction bunching strategy (as discussed in Chapter 13). Deduction bunching *can* be done without a donor-advised fund: just make large donations every several years rather than smaller donations every year. So again, the donor-advised fund isn't providing any additional tax savings. But with a donor-advised fund you can make the tax/budgeting decision now and decide which charity ultimately gets the money later. Again, not a *tax* benefit, but a real *administrative* benefit.

Anonymity, if Desired

The overwhelming majority of donations made in the U.S. are not anonymous. And that's not terribly surprising. Most people *want* to be thanked. Plus, the simplest ways of donating to a charity (i.e., writing a check or pulling out the credit card) result in donations that aren't anonymous.

But if you want to remain anonymous for any reason (even if that reason is just to stay off the mailing lists), donor-advised funds can be helpful. That's because, when you make a grant from the fund to a charity of your choosing, you can select whether the grant will be anonymous or not. If you choose to remain anonymous, the charity would see, for example, that the donation came from Fidelity Charitable, but they wouldn't know who the actual original donor was. The donor-advised fund serves as a middleman, shielding your identity.

Simplification of Donating Securities

As discussed in Chapter 12, when you donate assets that a) are not held in retirement accounts such as an IRA, b) have gone up in value, and c) you have owned for longer than one year, you get to claim an itemized deduction for the current market value of the asset *and* you do not have to pay tax on the appreciation. As such, donating such appreciated assets can be a very tax-savvy way to give.

But many charities, especially smaller ones, simply aren't set up to accept donations of anything other than cash.

Donor-advised funds, on the other hand, are ideally situated to accept donations of securities, given that they're often run by financial institutions. In fact, if your donor-advised fund is through the same company where you have your taxable brokerage account, the web interface will generally have a very easy way to simply select shares for donation and have them transferred to the donor-advised fund. And then from there, the fund can make a cash grant to the charity of your choosing.

What About Tax-Free Growth?

Sometimes people promote donor-advised funds by mentioning that they allow the money to remain invested and grow, tax-free, prior to being distributed to the ultimate charity. But this benefit is just an illusion. If you donate money directly to a charity, that charity can invest the money, and any gains that they earn will be tax-free (because they're a tax-exempt organization).

Some people counter that most charities would not choose to invest the money (i.e., they would spend it shortly after receiving the donation). That may be true of course. But when you donate to a donor-advised fund and invest the money for some years, rather than donating immediately to the ultimate charity, all that is achieved in this regard is that you have *deprived* the charity of the *choice* to spend the money immediately. In most cases I would argue that the charity itself has better knowledge of its goals, plans, and financial circumstances than the donor would have and is therefore in a better position to make this decision.

Drawbacks of Donor-Advised Funds

While donor-advised funds do offer useful administrative benefits, there are drawbacks as well.

The first downside is the cost. In addition to the costs of the investments held in the account, donor-advised funds typically charge an administrative fee as well. For instance, as of this writing, the donor-advised funds from Vanguard, Fidelity, and Schwab each charge an administrative fee of 0.6% per year (with a lower percentage for larger accounts). That said, the smaller the balances in question—and the shorter the length of time that money is left there—the less important such costs are.

A second potential downside of donor-advised funds is that they often impose a minimum grant size (i.e., for when you direct money to be distributed from the fund to a charity). In some cases though, that minimum is very modest (e.g., $50 at Fidelity or Schwab, as of this writing).

A final downside is simply that donor-advised funds cannot be the recipient for a qualified charitable distribution from a traditional IRA. So if you want to take advantage of QCDs, you must, at that time, determine the ultimate charity to which you want the money to go.

Chapter 14 Simple Summary

- A donor-advised fund is a non-profit entity, likely run by a financial institution. From a tax standpoint, contributions to the fund count as charitable contributions. After contributing to the fund, you can control how that money will be invested, to what charity/charities it will ultimately be distributed, and when those distributions will occur.

- Donor-advised funds do not provide any unique tax benefits. Any tax savings you get from contributing to a donor-advised fund could be achieved through donating directly to some other charity instead.

- Donor-advised funds do, however, provide certain administrative benefits, such as separating the tax planning decision (how much to donate in a given year) from the ultimate decision of how much to give to which charity.

- Donor-advised funds also make it easier to donate appreciated securities

- Donor-advised funds also make it easy to donate anonymously.

CHAPTER FIFTEEN

The Roth Question(s)

Many decisions relating to retirement accounts are largely a function of tax rates. For instance, when choosing between contributing to a Roth account or a tax-deferred ("traditional") account, it usually makes sense to make tax-deferred contributions if your current marginal tax rate is greater than the marginal tax rate you expect to pay on these dollars when they come out of the account later. Conversely, Roth contributions make sense if you think your current marginal tax rate is less than the future marginal tax rate.

Similarly, Roth conversions (in which you move money from a tax-deferred account into a Roth account and pay tax on the amount moved) generally make sense whenever your current marginal tax rate is less than the rate you expect to pay on these dollars when they come out of the account later.

But once you realize that a major part of the assets are likely to still be in the account upon your death, an important factor is the tax rate that would be paid by the party or parties that inherit the tax-deferred assets.

If it's your kids who are getting the assets, those questions become largely a matter of how their tax rate(s) would compare to your current tax rate. (So, for example, if your kids are high-earning physicians, Roth conversions are likely to make more sense than if your kids have careers with more modest earnings.)

Conversely, if it's a non-profit organization that is going to be getting the assets (or a significant portion of the assets), Roth conversions probably don't make sense. Tax-exempt charities don't have to pay tax on distributions from tax-deferred accounts. Note that this is true regardless of whether the charity is receiving the tax-deferred assets during your lifetime via qualified charitable distributions or upon your death via the beneficiary designations on your accounts. In either case, the greater the portion that you're going to give to charity, the less sense Roth conversions make. (Essentially, a conversion means paying tax now to avoid paying tax later. But tax-deferred dollars going to charity would face a 0% tax rate later anyway.)

Similarly, tax-deferred *contributions* become more valuable the greater your charitable intent—you're getting a deduction now, and (at least a portion of) the money will come out of the account later, tax-free to the charity.

In short, the greater your charitable intent:

- The less sense Roth contributions make,
- The less sense Roth conversions make, and
- The more sense tax-deferred contributions make.

Chapter 15 Simple Summary

- Roth conversions (and Roth contributions rather than tax-deferred contributions) make sense when your current marginal tax rate is lower than the marginal tax rate that you expect will be paid when these dollars come out of the account later.

- If your kids or other loved ones are going to be inheriting much of the account balances, their future tax rate(s) becomes a major factor in the decision.

- The greater your plans for charitable giving, the less sense Roth contributions and Roth conversions make, because the more likely it is that some of these dollars will have a 0% tax rate in the future, when they go to a tax-exempt nonprofit organization.

CHAPTER SIXTEEN

(State) Estate Taxes

Even among those fortunate enough to have "more than enough," few households will be affected by the federal estate tax these days, with its $12,920,000 exclusion as of 2023 (and double that for a married couple).

But there are some states (12, as of this writing) that have their own estate tax, and in some cases the exclusion amount is much lower. For example, Oregon's estate tax applies to the amount by which an estate exceeds $1,000,000. In Massachusetts, any estate over $1,000,000 has to pay estate tax, and it has to pay the tax on nearly the whole amount, not just the amount by which the estate exceeds the threshold. Washington state has an estate tax for estates over $2,193,000. It's worth taking the time to look up the rules specific to your state.

If your state has such a tax, depending on the threshold amount, the accompanying rules, and your projected assets, there could be lots of planning implications.

It might be a big point in favor of gifting to loved ones during your lifetime or donating to charity (either during your lifetime or via bequest). At the federal level, annual gifts to individuals up to a certain limit do not count against your lifetime estate/gift tax exclusion. That may be true for your state as well. And as far as charitable giving, at the federal level donations during your life and charitable bequests both reduce your taxable estate. Again, that may apply for your state as well.

Being subject to an estate tax can be a point in favor of creating certain types of trusts. This is because assets owned by an irrevocable trust are generally not considered part of your taxable estate. The transfer of assets to such a trust *will* generally count against your lifetime estate/gift tax exclusion. But for assets that are expected to appreciate over time, making the transfer now may be preferable to the transfer occurring later, at your death, at a presumably-higher value. For a married couple, trusts can also be helpful for making sure that *each* spouse gets to take advantage of the applicable estate tax exclusion amount in the state in question. (If you think either of these points might be relevant to you, speaking with an estate planning attorney is a good idea.)

Being subject to an estate tax is often a point in favor of Roth conversions, because when you do a conversion, the size of the taxable estate is reduced. (For example, after a given year's conversion you may be left with $80,000 in a Roth IRA rather than $100,000 in a traditional IRA, which is a good thing as far as estate tax goes.)

Chapter 16 Simple Summary

- Some states impose an estate tax with a much lower threshold than the federal estate tax.

- If your estate is likely to be subject to an estate tax (whether at the federal or state level), that's often a point in favor of: gifting during your lifetime, donating to charity (either during your lifetime or as a bequest), contributing assets to certain types of trusts, or doing Roth conversions. Speaking with an estate planning professional in your state is likely to be worthwhile.

CHAPTER SEVENTEEN

Developing a Workable Plan

We've spent the last several chapters discussing a bunch of tax planning strategies. But how do we merge them together into a comprehensive, workable plan?

In short, the plan must answer three questions regarding how you use your assets every year:

- Which assets should be used to satisfy the desired level of spending?
- Which assets should be used to satisfy the desired level of gifting (i.e., to individuals)?
- Which assets should be used to satisfy the desired level of charitable donations?

And the plan must answer two questions regarding your bequests:

- Which assets should be left to individuals?
- Which assets should be left to charity?

Which Dollars to Spend First Every Year

There's a common refrain in retirement planning that you want to spend from tax-deferred accounts when your marginal tax rate is low (as is often the case in years after you retire but before Social Security and RMDs kick in). It's true that it's better to spend from tax-deferred accounts than from Roth accounts when your tax rate is low. But there are other dollars that you want to spend first every year.

Let's consider an example. Imagine that, in a given month, you're trying to decide from which account to draw your next $1,000 of spending. And let's also imagine that, so far this year, your taxable income has not yet fully offset your standard deduction and credits for the year. In other words, you currently have a marginal tax rate of 0%.

The obvious approach—let's call it Option A—is to take the $1,000 out of your traditional IRA. Option A sounds pretty good, because this would be a tax-deferred distribution that's *completely* tax-free. That sounds like as a good a time as any to spend from a traditional IRA, right?

Probably not. Because there's likely an Option B: spend $1,000 from your regular taxable checking account and do a $1,000 Roth conversion.

In each case:

- You have spent $1,000,
- You have removed $1,000 from your traditional IRA, and
- You have incurred no tax bill.

But with Option A, the remaining $1,000 is in your taxable checking account, whereas with Option B the remaining $1,000 is now in a Roth IRA. In almost every case, you'd rather have $1,000 in a Roth IRA than in a taxable account, because further earnings in the Roth will generally be tax-free.

And a key point here is that this same concept applies for larger spending amounts and for higher tax rates.

In short, if you have taxable-account assets that you can spend without generating any tax cost, it makes sense to spend those assets before spending retirement account assets. And if, when following such a plan, you have low-tax-rate space in a given year that you wouldn't otherwise be using up, you can fill that space with Roth conversions.

In other words, every year before spending any dollars from retirement accounts (other than RMDs), you first want to spend from:

- Checking account dollars and
- Assets in taxable accounts that have cost basis at least equal to their current value.

When I say, "checking account dollars," I mean everything already in checking (and savings) accounts, as well as everything that automatically gets deposited into those accounts. That includes wage income, Social Security income, pension/annuity income, interest and dividends from holdings in taxable accounts, and RMDs from tax-deferred accounts.

Just to reiterate, the idea is to first spend from any assets that are not in retirement accounts and for which there would be no *further* tax-cost as a result of spending those dollars. And when following such a plan, if you have low-tax-rate space that isn't getting used, fill up that space with Roth conversions.

Also, to be clear, this is not a discussion of *how much* to spend each year. For some people, it does not make sense to spend all of those dollars every year (so some dollars will get reinvested). And for other people, the intended total level of spending exceeds the categories above, so it then becomes a question of whether to spend from tax-deferred accounts, spend from Roth accounts, or liquidate taxable assets for which there *would* be a tax cost.

I find that for clients in the "more than enough" set of circumstances, spending next from tax-deferred assets is often, but not always, what makes sense, in order to preserve Roth assets for heirs and to preserve appreciated taxable assets for the step-up in basis that heirs would later receive. (When a person inherits a taxable asset, their basis in that asset is "stepped up to" the fair market value of the asset as of the date of the owner's death—thereby allowing the appreciation up to the date of death to go entirely untaxed.)

Which Assets to Give (to Individuals) Every Year

When gifting to individuals (i.e., not charities) during your lifetime, the best dollars to use are largely the same as the best dollars to spend each year (i.e., usually checking account dollars as well as, in some cases, other dollars in taxable accounts). But there are two additional caveats.

First, gifting an appreciated taxable asset can be unwise in some cases, because it eliminates the step-up in basis that the recipient would otherwise have gotten if you held the asset and let them eventually inherit it.[1]

Second, with regard to a taxable asset that's currently worth *less* than what you paid for it, it's usually preferable to first sell it, claim the loss, and gift the resulting cash rather than gifting the asset.

---

[1] One noteworthy case in which it *does* make sense to gift appreciated taxable assets is when the recipient will be able to sell the asset and have the gain taxed as a long-term capital gain at a 0% tax rate. The rules regarding cost basis for assets received as a gift are complicated, so be sure to consult with a tax professional.

Which Assets to Donate Every Year

When choosing between qualified charitable distributions or donating taxable assets, one advantage of QCDs is that you can take advantage of them while claiming the standard deduction. In contrast, donations from taxable assets (including regular checking account dollars) give you an itemized deduction. And itemized deductions are only valuable to the extent that they (in total) exceed the standard deduction for the year.

QCDs also have the advantage that they reduce your adjusted gross income, which can sometimes produce additional beneficial results, such as allowing you to qualify for another deduction or credit or bringing your income below a particular threshold for determining Medicare premiums. In contrast, the itemized deduction from donating taxable assets does not reduce your AGI and therefore will not produce any such effects.

With regard to donating taxable assets, donating appreciated assets that you have owned for longer than one year is strictly better than donating other taxable account dollars (e.g., cash in a checking account). As discussed in Chapter 12, that's because you get to claim an itemized deduction for the current market value of the assets, while not having to pay tax on the appreciation.

To briefly summarize, the typical order of preference for donations each year is:

1. Donating via QCDs (if you're at least age 70.5),
2. Donating appreciated taxable assets with a holding period longer than one year,
3. Donating taxable account cash (e.g., checking/savings balances),
4. Donating appreciated taxable assets that you have held for one year or less,
5. Donating Roth IRA dollars (or donating traditional IRA dollars if you are younger than 70.5), and finally
6. Donating taxable assets where the current market value is less than your cost basis. (This option is unwise because your deduction is limited to the market value, and you don't get to claim a loss for the decline in value. Better to sell the asset, claim the capital loss, then donate the resulting cash.)

Which Assets to Leave to Whom

Tax-deferred accounts are the ideal asset for leaving to charity, because the charity doesn't have to pay any tax on the money, whereas any individual would have to pay tax as distributions are taken from the account.

And for the opposite reason, Roth accounts should go to a human rather than to charity. That is, a charity has no reason to prefer Roth dollars over tax-deferred dollars, whereas your kids (or grandkids) definitely *would* prefer Roth dollars.

Taxable assets work well for either party. Again, any assets are tax-free to a tax-exempt charity. And any humans who inherit taxable assets will receive a step-up in basis, thereby allowing them to sell the assets immediately (if desired) and incur little to no tax.

EXAMPLE: Aisha has decided that she wants to allocate her estate as follows: 40% to her children, 10% to her grandchildren, and 50% to charity.

Her assets are roughly broken down as: 40% tax-deferred accounts, 25% taxable brokerage accounts, 15% Roth IRA, 20% real estate (her home).

How should she divvy up those assets to meet the desired bequest allocation? Rather than taking a pro-rata approach, the ideal solution would probably be:

- The tax-deferred assets (40% of the total assets) go to charity,
- A portion of the taxable assets (10% of the total assets) goes to charity,
- Another portion of the taxable assets (10% of the total assets) goes to the grandkids,
- The rest of the taxable assets (including the home) as well as the Roth IRA go to the kids (40% of the total assets).

Again, the idea is: prioritize Roth for humans, prioritize tax-deferred for charity.

Bequests of Illiquid Assets

If you own an asset that generates income and which is illiquid (i.e., difficult to sell), I'd encourage you to consider leaving it to just one party. (Common examples of such assets would include a small business, the copyright to a book, or certain real estate.) When such assets are split by percentage among multiple parties, the ongoing income can force the estate to remain open (in order to distribute the income appropriately among the applicable parties) until the asset is sold. And if it's a difficult asset to sell, that could be an extended period of time.

Of course, if the goal is to leave equal shares of your estate to multiple parties, leaving an asset to only one of those parties would mean some other adjustments have to be made. And that can be a challenge, given that it can be hard to determine the value of the illiquid asset. Speaking with an estate planning attorney can be very valuable in these cases.

Chapter 17 Simple Summary

- Each year it usually makes sense to spend first from income (Social Security, wages, pension, interest and dividends from taxable holdings), required minimum distributions from tax-deferred accounts, and by selling taxable-account assets for which your cost basis is at least equal to the current value.

- Be careful about gifting (to individuals) taxable assets with a market value above or below your cost basis.

- For donations during your lifetime, QCDs are typically most attractive (once you qualify by being at least age 70.5), followed by donations of appreciated taxable assets.

- For charitable bequests, first use tax-deferred assets, then taxable assets, then Roth assets. For bequests to individuals, follow the opposite order (Roth, then taxable, then tax-deferred).

- For illiquid assets that generate income, it may be best to leave them to a single beneficiary.

PART FOUR

Finding Professional Assistance

CHAPTER EIGHTEEN

Working with an Attorney

We've covered a lot of ground, but there is still a dizzying array of estate planning topics that we have not discussed—topics about which an attorney would be able to give you valuable guidance. Some of the factors that would point in favor of hiring an attorney would include:

- You do not have your basic estate planning documents in place (i.e., will, financial power of attorney, advance healthcare directive)—or those documents were prepared long ago and are in need of an update.
- Your estate plan includes a trust or you suspect that it should include a trust.
- You have minor or disabled adult children who would inherit significant assets upon your death.
- You have one or more children with somebody other than your spouse—or he/she has

one or more children with somebody other than you.

- You expect that your (or your spouse's) estate will be subject to federal estate tax or your state's estate or inheritance tax.

One easy place to begin the search is simply with a Google search for estate planning attorneys in your area. The attorney doesn't *necessarily* have to be local, but somebody local will have better knowledge of your state's laws.

Another good approach is to ask around. Some people you might want to ask for a referral would include:

- Anybody in your social circle whom you know has similar financial circumstances.
- Any attorneys you know, with other areas of expertise.
- Any CPAs or other financial professionals you know.

It's critical to find an attorney with the right specialty. An attorney specializing in intellectual property law, for example, is not going to have the expertise you need. (Though again, such an attorney probably *would* be a good person to email to request a referral to an estate planning attorney.)

One quick but important step to take before officially engaging an attorney is to check the state bar association's website, to confirm that the attorney is currently licensed in your state.

For any attorney you're considering, be sure to explicitly ask: what experience do you have in dealing with clients in situations like mine?

It's also important to ask about their fees, including questions such as whether the initial consultation is free and what services are included for the stated fee.

If you're working with an attorney who charges hourly, have your records ready at hand and have a list of prepared questions. Being efficient will save you time and money. (Note that the same goes for working with any tax professional or financial planner who charges hourly.)

Chapter 18 Simple Summary

- If you have not already done so, engaging an attorney to help with your estate planning is very likely to be beneficial.

- Before engaging an attorney, be sure to ask about their relevant experience and get details as to their fees.

CHAPTER NINETEEN

Working with a Financial Planner

When it comes to finding somebody to provide financial advice, the first thing that confuses (and surprises) many people is that the term financial advisor doesn't have any legal meaning at all. Anybody can refer to himself or herself as a financial advisor. A person who refers to himself or herself as a financial advisor might, from a regulatory perspective, actually be any of a few different things: an investment adviser representative, an insurance agent, a registered representative, or none of the above.

Registered Investment Adviser (RIA)

A **registered investment adviser** (RIA) is an entity (a person or a business) that provides investment advice for a fee. An **investment adviser representative** (IAR) is a person who works for an RIA and provides advice on behalf of the RIA.

Registered investment advisers (and representatives thereof) have a fiduciary duty to their clients. That is, they're required by law to put the client's interests ahead of their own. Unfortunately, the reality is that there are some RIAs who do not actually live up to a fiduciary standard, and regulatory enforcement of this standard has historically been lackluster, to say the least. So a certain level of self-education is still necessary, in order for you to be able to understand what the advisor is recommending and why.

Registered Representative

A **registered representative** (also known as a broker or stockbroker) is a salesperson for a broker-dealer (i.e., a brokerage firm). Registered representatives are generally paid a commission. Despite providing advice, they do not (usually) have to be RIAs, because the advice they provide is considered to be solely incidental to the business as a broker (i.e., the business of selling investments).

Though regulation on this topic is currently evolving, in some circumstances registered representatives are only held to a "suitability" standard rather than a fiduciary standard. That is, they are not always required to put the client's interests first.

When you see, "securities offered by...." on a website or other piece of marketing material, you are dealing with a registered representative.

Certified Public Accountant (CPA)

The **certified public accountant** (CPA) designation is a license (at the state level). But, roughly speaking, the only things that CPAs are allowed to do which other people are not allowed to do are:

- Provide auditing (or similar) services, and
- Use the "CPA" letters after their name.

So if you're looking for personal financial services, it's very unlikely that you *need* somebody who is a CPA. That said, the CPA designation can be relevant, as it means that the person has a certain level of expertise with tax and other financial topics.

Enrolled Agent (EA)

Enrolled agents are tax professionals federally licensed by the IRS. To become an enrolled agent, a professional must pass a comprehensive exam covering a wide range of tax-related topics.

There is no service for which an enrolled agent is the only authorized provider. But like the

CPA designation, the EA designation does indicate a meaningful level of expertise.

Certified Financial Planner (CFP)

The **certified financial planner** (CFP) designation is not actually a license. The entity that provides this designation (Certified Financial Planner Board of Standards, Inc, generally referred to as the "CFP Board") is a private entity rather than a governmental entity.

From a legal standpoint, all this designation means is that the person is allowed to use the registered trademark "CFP professional" to describe himself/herself and use the registered trademark "CFP" letters after his/her name.

So from a legal standpoint, this designation is not important at all. That is, there's no service at all for which it's legally necessary for the service provider to be a CFP. However, the CFP designation does mean that the person a) has passed an exam that covers quite a bit of financial planning material and b) has a meaningful amount of experience providing one or more financial planning services.

What Type of Professional is Right for You?

An important point to understand is that somebody can work in more than one of the above roles. For example, it's common to see people who are both IARs and registered representatives. That is, they provide advice for a fee, and they also sell products for a commission. And that person might also have the CPA or CFP designations—or not.

Before searching for individual professionals, take a few minutes to consider three questions:

1. What services do you want?
2. What credentials do you want?
3. How do you want to pay for those services?

Are you looking for comprehensive financial planning? Then it's probably best to find somebody who is an RIA (or representative thereof). The CFP designation would be great to see. But it isn't entirely necessary.

Are you looking specifically for somebody to do a certain type of tax planning for you? Then a CPA, tax attorney, or enrolled agent could be a good fit—or even a CFP, if they happen to specialize in that particular area.

For most aspects of estate planning, the best professional to work with is an attorney.

Just because somebody has the right designation(s) doesn't mean he or she is necessarily a good fit for what you need. Experience matters as well. Before hiring a particular professional, take the time to explicitly ask about their experience helping clients with situations like yours.

Compensation is also important. If you're looking for a one-time engagement or periodic advice on an as-needed basis, it likely makes sense to find a professional who charges hourly or project-based fees and who *usually* works in such a manner, rather than a professional who prefers to work with clients who have ongoing needs and who are happy to pay an ongoing annual fee. (Please note though that I have a clear conflict of interest on this topic, as I myself am a financial professional who charges on an hourly basis.)

Conversely, if you want somebody who will manage your portfolio for you or who will proactively reach out to you on a regular basis about various financial planning topics, you should probably work with somebody who charges a monthly or quarterly retainer. That retainer could be a flat fee or an asset-based fee. (You can do the math yourself to determine which will cost less, given your circumstances.)

On the topic of compensation, I would also encourage you to ask any financial professional you're considering working with about the *total* costs you would be paying on your portfolio, if you choose to work with them. The key point here is that certain professionals (in particular, insurance agents and registered representatives) may not charge you any fee specifically for the advice that they give you, but they might put your money into certain investment products that pay them a commission and/or ongoing annual compensation. And those products carry higher costs for you as the investor.

Researching Disclosures

Before working with a financial professional, it's wise to check whether they have any relevant disciplinary history. The Financial Industry Regulatory Authority (FINRA) is the self-regulatory organization that regulates the brokerage industry. FINRA has a tool called BrokerCheck (which, as of this writing, can be found at brokercheck.finra.org) that you can use to search for a financial professional by name to see if they have any "disclosures."

Disclosures include things such as findings that the person violated securities laws or regulations, customer complaints alleging that the person committed theft or fraud, or certain types of financial-related civil litigation against the person.

While FINRA is in charge of regulating brokers (i.e., registered representatives) rather than investment advisers, the BrokerCheck search does work for investment adviser representatives as well.

Do take this information with a grain of salt though. A lack of disclosures should not be seen as a definitive indication that this person always puts their clients' interests first. And, conversely, the presence of a disclosure isn't necessarily a reason not to work with a person. (After all, some disclosures are simply *allegations* rather than *findings* of anything.) But a disclosure is a reason to, at least, find out more information about the event in question.

Chapter 19 Simple Summary

- Registered investment advisers (and representative thereof) have a fiduciary duty to their clients. This duty is not, however, very strictly enforced most of the time, so it is still important to educate yourself about the pros and cons of whatever a particular professional recommends to you.

- Certain designations (e.g., CFP, CPA, or EA) demonstrate knowledge about certain topics, but they are not legally necessary.

- Before engaging a financial professional, be sure to ask about their relevant experience and get details as to their fees and the total costs you will pay.

- If you want ongoing financial planning and investment management, a planner who charges a periodic retainer is going to be a better fit. If you want one-time or as-needed advice, a planner who charges hourly or per-project is likely to be a better fit.

- Before working with a professional, do a search on BrokerCheck to see if they have any relevant disciplinary history.

CONCLUSION

Mission Accomplished. Now What?

The overwhelming majority of financial media and financial advice deals with the topic of accumulating enough savings to cover your expenses throughout your lifetime.

Perhaps you have recognized that you have already accomplished that mission; you already have more than enough. Or perhaps you're *on track* to end up with more than enough, and you're planning ahead.

Or perhaps you think of yourself as having "enough" rather than "more than enough." Even in those cases, if you're spending at a conservative rate from your savings (which is almost a necessity, given that it's impossible to know how long you'll live, what investment returns you'll get, or what major expenses will arise), the reality is that you're unlikely to fully deplete your assets during your lifetime. That is, "enough" ultimately turns out to be "more than enough," most of the time.

And that raises one obvious, important question: who gets the money? If you're not going to use all of your money during your lifetime, to whom should it go?

Maybe you intend for the money to go to your offspring or other loved ones. Maybe you intend for it to go to charity. Most people I speak with tell me that a combination of the two is the answer that ends up feeling right. What I find—probably to nobody's surprise—is that people whose loved ones are already financially secure are more likely to leave a greater portion of their assets to charity.

By discussing your bequest plan with your kids (or other heirs) now, you give yourself the opportunity to make adjustments based on input. And you give yourself the opportunity to explain your reasoning to them. In addition, for any portion of the inheritance that your heirs would give to charity, you can instead leave those amounts directly to charity from tax-deferred accounts, resulting in tax savings for the ultimate recipient.

Sadly, a common pattern among families in which the parents are financially successful is that the parents do little donating or giving during their lifetimes. And by the time the parents have died, the "kids" are already retired. And at that point, the inheritance has no major effect on their happiness or standard of living. Donations and gifts could have been made earlier. Relatively modest gifts received early in life are often more impactful than larger inheritances received later in life.

But many people, understandably, find it difficult to shift into spending/giving-from-savings mode after decades of working hard to *accumulate* savings. You may find it more comfortable to follow the same guideline you've followed all along: limit your spending to an amount that's less than your income (i.e., dividends, interest, Social Security, and any pension or earned income). Never spend any principal, in other words. That's fine, if doing so allows you to better achieve your goals. But unless you have gone out of your way to craft a portfolio of high-yield bonds and high-dividend stocks, it is generally OK to spend somewhat more from your portfolio than just the interest and dividends that it pays.

The realization that you have, or are on track to have, more than enough financial resources also brings up a list of other questions.

For instance: can your investment portfolio achieve anything other than simply delivering financial returns? For mutual funds that you own (or are considering buying) I would encourage you to research the fund's policy for voting its shares, to check whether that policy matches your own values. You can find that policy in the fund's Statement of Additional Information. I would also point out that when a fund excludes a company from its portfolio, it gives up the opportunity to influence that company's behavior via shareholder votes.

And how can you achieve the greatest impact with your charitable giving? Of course, different people will make different judgements about what types of "good" are most important and most urgent. For any specific causes that are important to you, I would encourage you to spend some time researching multiple organizations before donating to any particular one, in order to see which might be the most likely to deliver the highest impact per dollar, for your particular charitable goals. For each organization, find out very specifically what it aims to accomplish, how exactly it intends to do that, and what evidence it can show of achievements to date.

Reassessing your asset allocation is another wise step to take, upon realizing that a significant portion of your portfolio will ultimately go to other parties. For instance, it might make sense to use a static, stock-oriented allocation, as would be typical of an endowment portfolio, rather than a more conservative allocation as is often recommended for retirees.

That "more than enough" realization also brings up a list of important tax planning considerations. In short, tax planning is very different when a major part of the assets will ultimately go to other parties via bequest or donation rather than being spent during your lifetime.

For charitable giving, donating appreciated taxable assets that you have held for longer than one year (e.g., shares of stock in a taxable brokerage account that have increased in value) is a very tax-efficient approach. You get an itemized deduction for the market value of the asset, and you do not have to pay any tax on the appreciation.

After reaching age 70.5, qualified charitable distributions (QCDs) are frequently an even better charitable giving method. QCDs allow you to donate assets from a traditional IRA directly to charity, allowing the charity to take advantage of the full value of the assets, because neither you nor the charity has to pay tax on the distribution. In addition, qualified charitable distributions count toward satisfying your required minimum distributions. So for any year in which you won't need your full RMD for spending, they are a very tax-efficient way to make use of the assets.

Similarly, for charitable bequests, tax-deferred assets (such as a traditional IRA) are ideal. When you leave tax-deferred assets to a nonprofit organization, the organization can take advantage of the full value of the assets. In contrast, if such assets are left to individuals, those beneficiaries can only use the amount that's left after taxes.

The best asset for gifting to individuals during your lifetime is typically plain-old checking account cash—which over time mostly comes from any income that is received each year (e.g., Social Security, pension income, earned income, RMDs, or interest/dividends from holdings in a taxable brokerage account).

As far as annual spending, the best assets to spend each year are checking account dollars, as well as any investments in taxable brokerage accounts where your cost basis is at least equal to the current market value. After spending any such dollars each year, the next-best dollars to spend are typically taxable assets for which the unrealized gain is modest.

Next in the order of priority is either Roth dollars or tax-deferred dollars, depending on how you think your current marginal tax rate compares to the marginal tax rate that the tax-deferred dollars would face later (i.e., whenever they come out of the account later, if you don't take them out now for spending). Note that this "later" tax rate may be your heirs' tax rate rather than your own. If your current marginal tax rate is lower than the anticipated future tax rate, spending from tax-deferred makes sense, whereas spending from Roth makes sense if the current tax rate is higher than the anticipated future tax rate.

For highly appreciated taxable assets which are not intended to be donated, it's often best to try to save them for a bequest, so that your heirs can receive a step-up in basis (thereby allowing the appreciation to go untaxed).

Donor-advised funds can provide benefits such as the ability to remain anonymous while making donations, if desired. In addition, they separate the tax-planning/budgeting decision (i.e., "I want to donate $X to charity this year") from the ultimate decision of which charities will get the money and when. This can be helpful if you intend to use a "deduction bunching" strategy. With such a strategy, you make a few (or several) years' worth of donations in a single year, in order to get a large itemized deduction in that year, while using the standard deduction in other years. With a donor-advised fund you can make a large contribution to the fund in one year, then dole it out to the ultimate charity recipients over time.

If your state imposes an estate tax with a lower threshold than the federal estate tax—or if you expect your estate to be subject to the federal estate tax—be sure to consult with a professional, as there are probably tax planning opportunities available to you.

If you're likely to leave behind a significant estate, working with an estate planning attorney is a good idea. That's *especially* true if you do not have your basic estate planning documents in place, if those documents are in need of an update, if you have minor or disabled adult children who would inherit significant assets upon your death, or if you have one or more children with somebody other than your spouse—or he/she has one or more children with somebody other than you.

Before hiring an attorney, tax professional, or financial planner, be sure to ask for detailed information as to the fees charged as well as what exactly you will receive for those fees.

If you're interested in working with a financial planner, thinking carefully about exactly what services you want can help narrow down the search.

If all you want is as-needed advice, a financial planner who charges on an hourly or per-project basis is likely to be the best fit. Conversely, if you want somebody who will manage your portfolio as well as provide ongoing guidance, working with a financial planner who charges an ongoing retainer is likely to be the best fit. (Whether an asset-based fee or a flat fee offers the best value will depend largely on the size of your portfolio.)

AFTERWORD

Our Most
Limited Resource

George Kinder—a financial planner and founder of the burgeoning field known as Life Planning—encourages people to reflect upon three questions.

The first question: imagine that you have all the money that you need for the rest of your life. What would you do with that? What would you do with your life?

For many people reading this book, this "imagine" scenario is reality already—or not terribly far from it. Even still, it's one thing to be in a financial position to be *able* to live like you have all the money that you need. It's another thing to actually live that way.

Second question: imagine that, during a routine doctor visit, your doctor informs you that you have a rare condition which means you only have five to ten years left to live. You won't ever feel sick. (Or you'll feel no worse than you feel now.) But you will have no warning of the moment of your death. What would you do with those five to ten years?

Third question: this time, your doctor shocks you with the news that you only have 24 hours left to live. This time the question isn't what do you do with the time, but rather what do you think and feel? What do you wish you had done? Who do you wish you had been?

Jordan Grumet, in his book *Taking Stock: A Hospice Doctor's Advice on Financial Independence, Building Wealth, and Living a Regret-Free Life,* writes that people at the end of their lives do indeed often express sentiments that fit the pattern of "I regret that I did not have the time/energy/courage to _____."

For you, what would be in that blank, as things stand right now?

For most people, the answers to this question will change over time. And the answers don't have to be big, world-changing goals in order to be valid. Your answer could be something very personal and simple like "I wish I had learned how to paint."

People sometimes choose not to pursue these goals because they're scared they won't succeed. But, per Grumet, the dying don't typically regret the things at which they tried and did not succeed. More often, they regret the things they didn't have the courage to try—or simply didn't bother to try.

Statistically, most people reading this book have well more than 24 hours left to live, and most will have more than 5-10 years left to live. Regardless, we have a finite amount of time. Time is our most limited resource.

If you were in a financial position where you had just *barely* enough to cover your bills every month, you'd be extremely careful about how you spend your money. Any spending that did not serve a critical purpose would be eliminated.

Money is so easily quantified. We can see precisely how much we have. And so it lends itself to careful spending.

I find that it's easier to accidentally or carelessly spend my time. Maybe you find the same thing to be true.

Dear reader, you just bought and read a whole book talking about how to allocate a resource of which you, likely, have "more than enough." (And I have spent quite a bit of time writing said book.)

Let's you and I both try to be as conscientious about how we allocate this other resource of which we surely do not have more than enough.

Acknowledgements

My thanks go to financial planners Allan Roth of Colorado Springs, Colorado and Elliott Appel of Madison, Wisconsin for sharing their expertise and providing valuable feedback. And thank you, as always, to my reliable editing team: Kalinda, Pat, and Debbi.

Also by Mike Piper

After the Death of Your Spouse: Next Financial Steps for Surviving Spouses

Can I Retire? How to Manage Your Retirement Savings, Explained in 100 Pages or Less

Social Security Made Simple: Social Security Retirement Benefits and Related Planning Topics Explained in 100 Pages or Less

Investing Made Simple: Investing in Index Funds Explained in 100 Pages or Less

Taxes Made Simple: Income Taxes Explained in 100 Pages or Less

LLC vs. S-Corp vs. C-Corp Explained in 100 Pages or Less

Independent Contractor, Sole Proprietor, and LLC Taxes Explained in 100 Pages or Less

Microeconomics Made Simple: Basic Microeconomic Principles Explained in 100 Pages or Less

Corporate Finance Made Simple: Corporate Finance Explained in 100 Pages or Less

About the Author

Mike is the author of several books as well as the popular blog ObliviousInvestor.com. He is a Missouri licensed CPA. Mike's writing has been featured in many places, including *The Wall Street Journal, Money, Forbes,* and *MarketWatch.* Mike is also the creator of the Open Social Security calculator, which has been featured in *The New York Times, The Wall Street Journal,* and elsewhere.

INDEX

Made in United States
North Haven, CT
28 April 2024

51862373R00088